Downtown 1

English for Work and Life

EDWARD J. MCBRIDE

THOMSON

HEINLE

Downtown 1
English for Work and Life
Edward J. McBride

Publisher, Adult and Academic: James W. Brown
Senior Acquisitions Editor, Adult and Academic: Sherrise Roehr
Director of Product Development: Anita Raducanu
Developmental Editor: Kasia McNabb
Developmental Editor: Jill Korey O'Sullivan
Senior Director of Marketing: Amy Mabley
Field Marketing Manager: Donna Lee Kennedy
Product Marketing Manager: Laura Needham
Editorial Assistant: Katherine Reilly

Senior Production Editor: Maryellen E. Killeen
Senior Print Buyer: Mary Beth Hennebury
Photo Researcher: Christina Micek
Indexer: Alexandra Nickerson
Design and Composition: Jan Fisher/Publication Services
Cover Design: Lori Stuart
Cover Art: Jean-Francois Allaux
Printer: Courier Corporation/Kendallville

Printed in the United States of America
1 2 3 4 5 6 7 8 9 10   09 08 07 06 05

For more information contact Thomson Heinle, 25 Thomson Place, Boston, MA 02210 USA, or you can visit our Internet site at elt.thomson.com

For permission to use material from this text or product, submit a request online at http://www.thomsonrights.com

Any additional questions about permissions can be submitted by email to thomsonrights@thomson.com

ISBN: 0-8384-4374-5
International Student Edition: 1-4130-1542-5

Library of Congress Cataloging-in-Publication Data
McBride, Edward J., 1950–
   Downtown : English for work and life / Edward J. McBride.
      p. cm.
   "Book 1."
   ISBN: 0-8384-4374-5 (alk. paper)
   1. English language--Textbooks for foreign speakers. 2. English language--Business English--Problems, exercises, etc. 3. Life skills--Problems, exercises, etc. I. Title.

PE1128.M225 2004
428.2'4'02465--dc22   2004047869

Dedication

To all the wonderful students who have given me, over the years, at least as much as I have given them.

Acknowledgements

The author and publisher would like the thank the following reviewers for the valuable input:

Elizabeth Aderman
New York City Board of Education
New York, NY

Jolie Bechet
Fairfax Community Adult School
Los Angeles, CA

Cheryl Benz
Georgia Perimeter College
Clarkston, GA

Chan Bostwick
Los Angeles Unified School District
Los Angeles, CA

Patricia Brenner
University of Washington
Seattle, WA

Clif de Córdoba
Roosevelt Community Adult School
Los Angeles, CA

Marti Estrin
Santa Rosa Junior College
Santa Rosa, CA

Judith Finkelstein
Reseda Community Adult School
Reseda, CA

Lawrence Fish
Shorefront YM-YWHA
English Language Program
Brooklyn, NY

Giang Hoang
Evans Community Adult School
Los Angeles, CA

Arther Hui
Mount San Antonio College
Walnut, CA

Renee Klosz
Lindsey Hopkins Technical
Education Center
Miami, FL

Carol Lowther
Palomar College
San Marcos, CA

Barbara Oles
Literacy Volunteers of
Greater Hartford
Hartford, CT

Pamela Rogers
Phoenix College
Phoenix, AZ

Eric Rosenbaum
BEGIN Managed Programs
New York, NY

Stan Yarbro
La Alianza Hispana
Roxbury, MA

Contents

Contents

Contents

Contents

EFF	CASAS	LAUSD Beginning	Florida LCP-A	Texas LCP-A
Many EFF skills are practiced in this chapter, with a particular focus on: • Gathering, analyzing, and using information • Working together • Using math to solve problems • Taking responsibility for learning • Learning through research	• **Lesson 1:** 0.1.2, 0.2.1, 2.3.1, 2.3.2 • **Lesson 2:** 0.2.4 • **Lesson 3:** 2.3.2, 2.7.1, 3.1.2, 4.1.6	**Competencies:** 3, 13, 25, 26, 27, 40, 55 **Grammar:** 1c, 14c	• **Lesson 1:** 08.01, 08.02, 08.03 • **Lesson 2:** 07.06 • **Lesson 3:** 02.04, 07.04, 08.03	• **Lesson 1:** 8.01, 8.02, 8.03, 15.03 • **Lesson 2:** 7.06 • **Lesson 3:** 2.04, 7.04, 8.03
Many EFF skills are practiced in this chapter, with a particular focus on: • Managing resources • Working together • Using math to solve problems • Solving problems and making decisions • Reflecting and evaluating	• **Lesson 1:** 0.2.4, 1.5.3, 1.8.1, 6.1.2 • **Lesson 2:** 0.2.4 • **Lesson 3:** 4.1.8, 4.5.1	**Competencies:** 12, 13, 51 **Grammar:** 2	• **Lesson 1:** 08.06, 15.05 • **Lesson 2:** 15.05 • **Lesson 3:** 02.01, 04.01	• **Lesson 1:** 7.06, 8.06 • **Lesson 2:** 15.08 • **Lesson 3:** 2.01, 4.01
Many EFF skills are practiced in this chapter, with a particular focus on: • Gathering, analyzing, and using information • Working together • Providing leadership • Guiding and supporting others • Seeking guidance and support from others • Speaking so others can understand • Listening actively • Solving problems and making decisions	• **Lesson 1:** 0.1.2, 1.1.3, 2.2.1, 2.2.5 • **Lesson 2:** 0.1.2 • **Lesson 3:** 4.1.8	**Competencies:** 22, 23a, 23b, 50, 51 **Grammar:** 1, 2, 12, 14a	• **Lesson 1:** 09.03, 12.02, 13.02 • **Lesson 2:** 14.01 • **Lesson 3:** 12.01	• **Lesson 1:** 9.03, 12.02, 13.02 • **Lesson 2:** 5.01, 5.03, 14.01 • **Lesson 3:** 12.01

Contents

Contents

EFF	CASAS	LAUSD Beginning	Florida LCP-A	Texas LCP-A
Many EFF skills are practiced in this chapter, with a particular focus on: • Managing resources • Creating and pursuing vision and goals • Using math to solve problems • Solving problems and making decisions • Planning • Reflecting and evaluating • Advocating and influencing	• **Lesson 1:** 0.1.2, 1.4.1 • **Lesson 2:** 0.1.3.1, 1.5.1, 1.5.2, 6.1.1 • **Lesson 3:** 0.2.2, 1.4.2, 2.1.8	**Competencies:** 1.4.1, 19, 38, 39 **Grammar:** 13b	• **Lesson 1:** 11.05 • **Lesson 2:** 08.05, 08.06 • **Lesson 3:** 06.01, 15.04, 15.06	• **Lesson 1:** 11.05 • **Lesson 2:** 8.05, 8.06 • **Lesson 3:** 5.04, 6.01, 15.06, 15.08
Many EFF skills are practiced in this chapter, with a particular focus on: • Exercising rights and responsibilities • Guiding and supporting others • Seeking guidance and support from others • Working within the big picture • Solving problems and making decisions • Cooperating with others • Advocating and influencing	• **Lesson 1:** 0.1.3, 0.1.4, 1.1.5, 3.1.1, 3.5.9, 6.6.4 • **Lesson 2:** 0.1.3, 3.1.2, 3.1.3, 3.3.2, 3.4.1, 4.4.1, 6.1.3 • **Lesson 3:** 0.1.2, 2.1.2, 2.5.1, 4.1.8	**Competencies:** 21, 29, 43, 44, 46, 50, 51, 57 **Grammar:** 13b	• **Lesson 1:** 07.01, 07.02, 07.03, 07.05 • **Lesson 2:** 07.02, 07.04, 07.05 • **Lesson 3:** 06.03, 07.03, 12.02	• **Lesson 1:** 7.01, 7.02, 7.03, • **Lesson 2:** 5.04, 7.04, 7.05 • **Lesson 3:** 6.03, 7.03, 12.02
Many EFF skills are practiced in this chapter, with a particular focus on: • Gathering, analyzing, and using information • Working together • Guiding and supporting others • Seeking guidance and support from others • Developing and expressing sense of self • Respecting others and valuing diversity • Using math to solve problems	• **Lesson 1:** 3.5.2, 6.7.2 • **Lesson 2:** 1.1.7, 1.2.1, 1.2.4, 1.3.8 • **Lesson 3:** 0.1.2, 0.1.3, 2.6.4	**Competencies:** 14a, 35, 37 **Grammar:** 3, 8, 15d	• **Lesson 1:** 05.03, 07.07 • **Lesson 2:** 11.01, 11.02 • **Lesson 3:** 15.05, 15.06	• **Lesson 1:** 5.03, 7.07 • **Lesson 2:** 11.01, 11.02 • **Lesson 3:** 15.08

Contents

Contents

To the Teacher

Attempting to learn a new language can often be challenging and even frustrating. But learning English should also be fun. That's the idea I was given by the wonderful administrator who hired me twelve years ago to teach my first ESL class. She took me aside as I was about to walk nervously into class for the first time. "Make your students comfortable," she said. "Make the class fun. And teach them what they really need to know."

Twelve years of teaching and about ten thousand students later, these simple, yet essential, ideas have become guiding pedagogical principles for me. In each of my classes, I have striven to teach students what they need to know, in a way that is both comfortable and enjoyable. Ultimately, that's the philosophy behind *Downtown*, too. The simplicity of the layout of each page, along with the logical, slow-paced progression of the material makes it a comfortable text for both teachers and students to use. I've included a wide variety of activities, as well as playful features like "Game Time" and a chapter-concluding cartoon, to make *Downtown* an enjoyable text to use. And, by developing the text with a focus on standards-based competencies, I've sought to teach students the information they most need to know.

This four-level, competency-based series is built around the language skills students need to function in both their everyday lives and in the workplace, while giving a good deal of attention to grammar. It is a general ESL text that pays more attention to work-related language needs than is typical. The goal of the text is to facilitate student-centered learning in order to lead students to real communicative competence.

The first page of each chapter of *Downtown* presents an overview of the material of the chapter in context, using a picture-dictionary format. This is followed by three lessons, with the third lesson focusing on work-related English. Many of the structures and key concepts are recycled throughout the lessons, with the goal of maximizing student practice. Each lesson is carefully scaffolded to progress from guided practice to more communicative activities in which students begin to take more control of their own learning.

Each chapter concludes with a Chapter Review, which provides material that practices and synthesizes the skills that students have been introduced to in the previous three lessons. The review culminates in a "Teamwork Task" activity. This activity gives students the opportunity to work together to apply the skills they have learned to complete a real world type of task. At the end of each chapter you will find a *Downtown* cartoon—a humorous, serial-style cartoon, which invites students to practice the vocabulary and grammar presented in the chapter.

Each chapter presents a variety of activities that practice grammar, as well as reading, writing, listening, and speaking skills. Problem-solving activities are also included in many lessons, and are particularly emphasized at the higher levels.

The material in **Downtown** is presented in real-life contexts. Students are introduced to vocabulary, grammar, and real-world skills through the interactions of a cast of realistic, multiethnic characters who function as parents, workers, and community members in their own "downtown" world.

My intention in developing **Downtown** was to provide an easy-to-use text, brimming with essential and enjoyable language learning material. I hope **Downtown** succeeds in this and that it helps to cultivate an effective and motivating learning atmosphere in your classroom. Please feel free to send me your comments and suggestions at the Heinle Thomson Web site: elt.thomson.com. Ancillary material includes Teacher's Editions, workbooks, audio cassettes/CDs, transparencies, and an ExamView Pro assessment CD-Rom containing a customizable test bank for each level.

Downtown: English for Work and Life

Downtown offers a well-balanced approach that combines a standards-based and a grammar-based syllabus. This gives English learners the comprehensive language skills they need to succeed in their daily lives, both at home and at work.

- **Picture dictionary-style chapter openers** introduce vocabulary in context and outline chapter goals.

- **Audio Tapes and CDs** enhance learning through dialogues, listening practice, readings, and pronunciation exercises.

Theme-based chapters include three lessons. The third lesson in each chapter focuses on the skills and vocabulary necessary for the workplace.

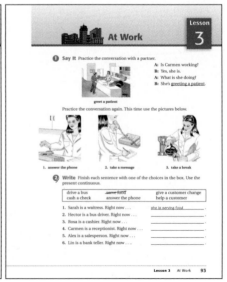

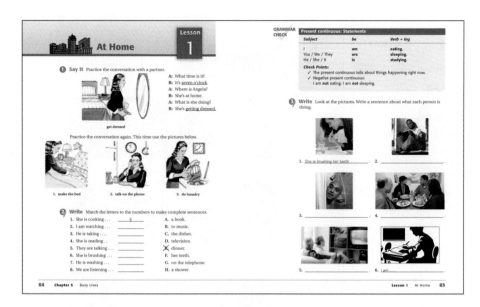

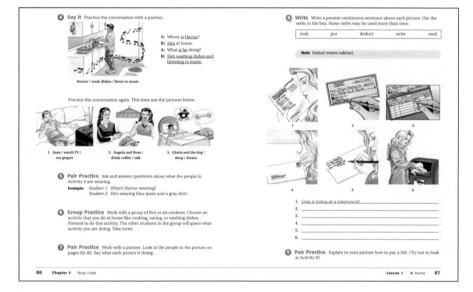

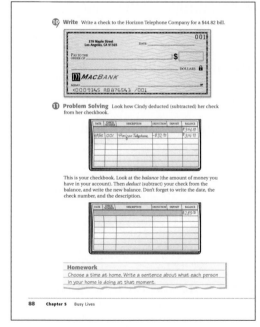

- **The strong grammar syllabus** supports the integrated language learning focus.

- **The lives of recurring characters provide the context** for a variety of activities such as *Grammar Check, Say It, Game Time,* and other communicative items.

- **Problem solving activities** engage students' critical thinking.

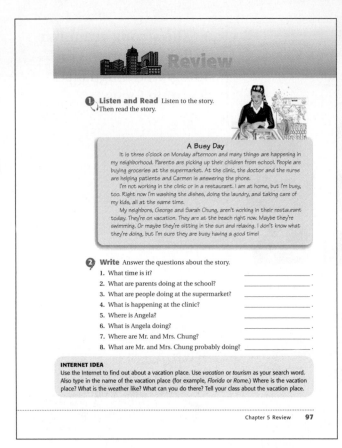

- **Review pages** practice all skills learned in the chapter and let students synthesize what they have learned.

- **A comic book story** at the end of each chapter reviews instructional content while providing the basis for role-play and team tasks.

Downtown Components

Audio Tapes and CDs enhance learning through dialogues, listening practice, readings, and pronunciation exercises.

Workbooks reinforce lessons and maximize student practice of key reading, writing, listening, speaking, and grammar points.

Transparencies can be used to introduce lessons, develop vocabulary, and stimulate expansion activities.

Assessment CD-ROM with *ExamView®Pro* allows teachers to create, customize, and correct tests and quizzes quickly and easily.

Teacher's Editions provide student book answers and teaching suggestions.

Alignment with the CASAS, SCANS, EFF Competencies and state standards supports classroom and program goals.

Photo Credits

Chapter 1
Pg. 5, TL: © Amy Etra / Photo Edit; TR: © Kathleen Kliskey-Geraghty/ Index; M: © Tony Freeman / Photo Edit; B: © Frank Siteman / Photo Edit
Pg. 13, All: © Hemera Photo Objects

Chapter 2
Pg. 24, TL: © Hemera Photo Objects; TCL: © Hemera Photo Objects; TCR: © Ryan McVay/ Photodisc/ Getty Images; TR: © Royalty-Free/Corbis; BL: © Siede Preis/ Photodisc/ Getty Images; BCL: © Hemera Photo Objects; BCR: © Hemera Photo Objects; BR: © David Young-Wolff/ Alamy
Pg. 26, TL: © Hemera Photo Objects; TR: © Ryan McVay/ Photodisc/ Getty Images
Pg. 26, B-All: © Hemera Photo Objects

Chapter 3
Pg. 48, All except bills and quarter: © Eric Antoniou Photography; Bills and quarter: © Comstock
Pg. 49, Pen: © Hemera Photo Objects; T-shirt: © John Coletti; Tie: © Hemera Photo Objects
Pg. 49, All except bills and quarter: © Eric Antoniou Photography; Bills and quarter: © Comstock

Chapter 4
Pg. 65, All: © Hemera Photo Objects
Pg. 67, Rosa: © David Young Wolff/ Photo Edit
Pg. 71, T: © Digital Vision/ Getty Images; BL: © The Thomson Corporation/Heinle Image Resource Bank; BM: © Stockbyte; BR: © Adam Crowley/ Photodisc/ Getty Images

Chapter 5
Pg. 85, TL: © Ariel Skelley/CORBIS; TR: © Gary Conner/ Index; ML: © Park Street/ Photo Edit; MR: © Mary Kay Denny/ Photo Edit; BL: © Jose Luis Pelaez/ Corbis
Pg. 90, T: © Joe McBride/ CORBIS; BL: © Superstock; BM: © Image Source Limited/ Index Stock Imagery
Pg. 92, T: © The Thomson Corporation/Heinle Image Resource Bank; BL: © Douglas Slone/ CORBIS; BM: © Royalty-Free/Corbis; BR: © Photolink/ Photodisc/ Getty Images
Pg. 94, T: © Tony Freeman / Photo Edit; BL: © Brand X Pictures / Alamy; BM: © Bob Daemmrich/Image Works; BR: © Royalty-Free/Corbis

Chapter 6
Pg. 111, TL: © Ryan McVay/ Photodisc/ Getty Images; TR: © Francisco Cruz/ Superstock; ML: © Andersen Ross/ Photodisc/ Getty Images; MR: © Allana Wesley White/CORBIS; BL: © David Young-Wolff / Alamy; BR: © Yann Arthus-Bertrand/CORBIS

Pg. 113, TL: © Royalty-Free/Corbis; BR: © Ryan McVay/ Photodisc/ Getty Images; BM: © Bill Stormont/CORBIS; BL: © Jeff Greenberg/ Index Stock Imagery
Pg. 115, T: © David Young Wolff/ Photo Edit; BR: © David Young Wolff/ Photo Edit; BM: © Walter Hodges/ Getty Images; BR: © Robert Brenner/ Photo Edit

Chapter 7
Pg. 125, T: © Craig Orsini/ Index Stock Imagery; All Others: © Hemera Photo Objects
Pg. 127, All: © Hemera Photo Objects Window: © Lawrence Sawyer/ Index

Chapter 8
Pg. 144, T: © Sean Justice/ Getty Images; BL: © Royalty-Free/Corbis; BM: © BananaStock, BR: © Christina Kennedy/ Photo Edit
Pg. 148, TL: © Henryk T. Kaiser/ Index; TML: © Yoav Levy/ Phototake/ Alamy; TMR: © Royalty-Free/Corbis; TR: © BananaStock
Pg. 149, T: © Michelle D. Bridwell/ Photo Edit; BR: © Park Street. Photo Edit; BL: © Michael Newman/ Photo Edit
Pg. 155, TL: © Arnulf Husmo/ Getty Images; TM: © Michael Newman/ Photo Edit; TR: © Lon C. Diehl/ Photo Edit

Chapter 9
Pg. 164, Steak: © Superstock; Milk: © Royalty-Free/Corbis; Potato chips: © Burke/Triolo Productions/ Foodpix; Oil: © Rachel Epstein/ Photo Edit; Candy: © Steven Mark Needham/Foodpix; All others: © Hemera Photo Objects
Pg. 165, Chicken: © Superstock; Cheese: © Spencer Jones/ PictureArts/CORBIS; All others: © Hemera Photo Objects
Pg. 169, Potato Chips: © Foodcollection/ Alamy, All Others: © Hemera Photo Objects
Pg. 173, Waitress: © Michael Newman/ Photo Edit; Cup of coffee: © Ryan McVay/ Photodisc/ Getty Images; Pizza: © Michael Rutherford/ Superstock; All others: © Hemera Photo Objects
Pg. 179, Jam: © John Foxx/ Alamy; Soup: © Bill Aron/ Photo Edit; Rice: © John Coletti; Popcorn: © Royalty-Free/Corbis; Cereal: © John Coletti

Chapter 10
Pg. 186, T: © Patrik Giardino/CORBIS; BL: © David Young-Wolff/Photo Edit; BM: © Roger Ressmeyer/ CORBIS; BR: © Kwame Zikomo/ Superstock
Pg. 187, TL: © Tony Freeman / Photo Edit, TR: © Antonio Mo/ Getty Images, BL: © FK PHOTO/ CORBIS; BR: © Don Smetzer/ Photo Edit

Personal Information

GOALS

- ✓ Spell your name
- ✓ Greet people
- ✓ Introduce yourself and others
- ✓ Identify family members
- ✓ Say your address and phone number
- ✓ Fill out an application form
- ✓ Address an envelope
- ✓ Use the alphabet and numbers
- ✓ Put names in alphabetical order
- ✓ Make statements with *be*
- ✓ Use possessive adjectives

CHAPTER 1

ENGLISH CLASS REGISTRATION
Hi.
My name is Angela.
This is my family.
13
14
1
STUDENT REGISTRATION FORM
2
Name: Alex Marenko
3
Address: 14150 Melrose Street
Hollywood, CA 90512
5
4
Telephone number: (213) 555-3452
7
6
8
9

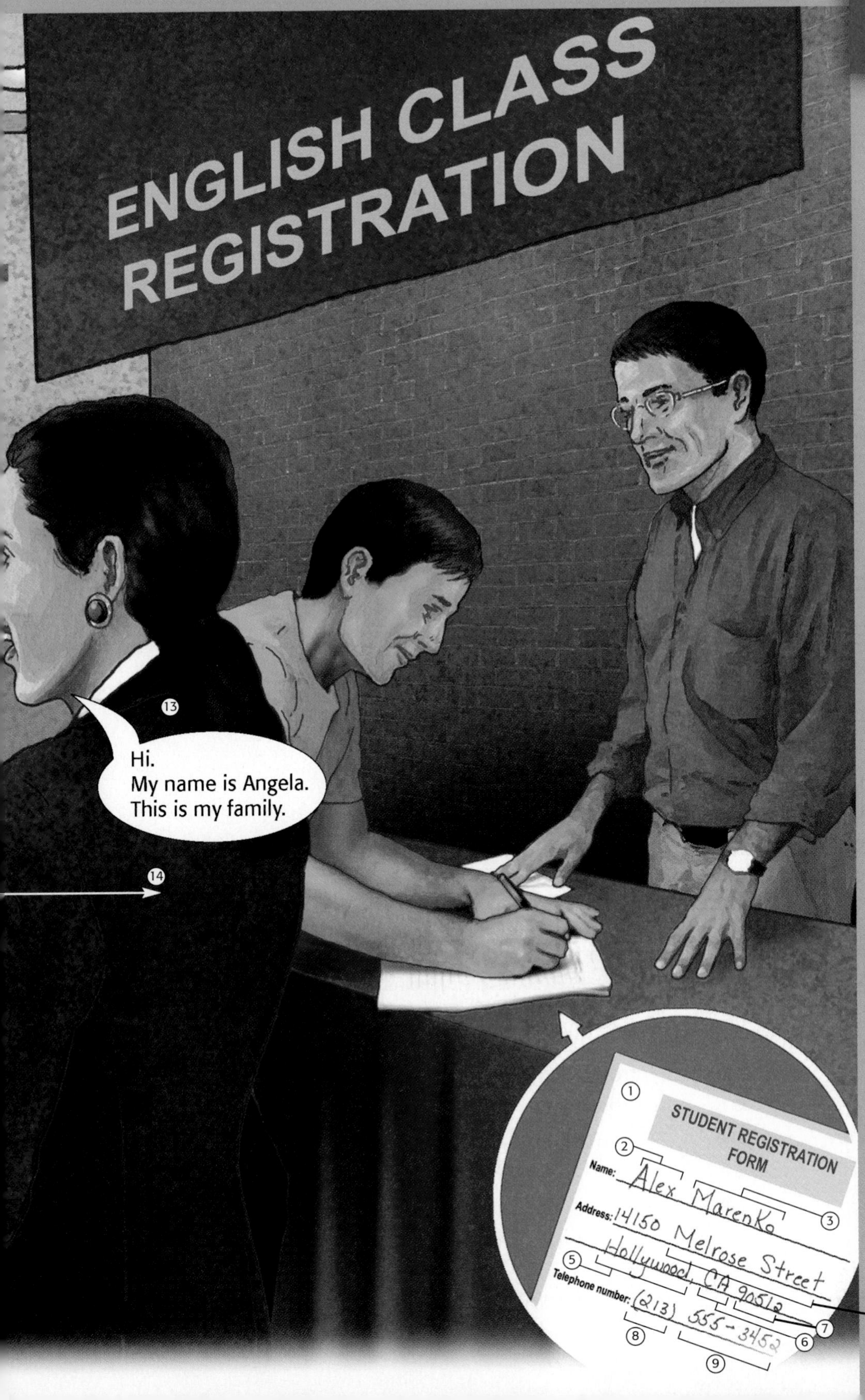

Listen

Listen and point to the words you hear. Then point to each item in the picture. Listen again and repeat each word.

1. form
2. first name
3. last name
4. street
5. city
6. state
7. zip code
8. area code
9. phone number
10. children
11. son
12. daughter
13. mother
14. wife
15. father
16. husband

Names and Greetings

1 **Pair Practice** Fill in the blanks with your own names. Then practice the conversation with your partner.

A: Good morning. My name is _____.

B: Hello. I am _____.

A: Nice to meet you.

B: Nice to meet you, too.

2 **Group Practice** Introduce yourself to three different students.

3 **Group Practice** Sit in a group of four students. Ask the other students in your group their names and where they are from.

Example: Student 1: What's your name?
Student 2: My name is _____.
Student 1: Where are you from?
Student 2: I am from _____.

GRAMMAR CHECK

Statements with *be*		
Subject	**be**	
I	**am**	from Mexico.
He/She/It	**is**	from Haiti.
You/We/They	**are**	from Japan.

4 **Say It** Practice the conversations with a partner.

A: What is his name?

B: His name is <u>Alex Marenko</u>.

A: Where is he from?

B: He is from <u>Russia</u>.

A: What is her name?

B: Her name is <u>Lin Tran</u>.

A: Where is she from?

B: She is from <u>Vietnam</u>.

Practice the conversation again. This time use the ID cards below.

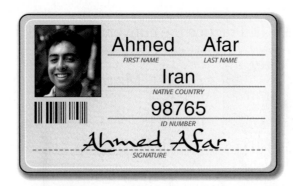

5 **Write** Fill in the blanks.

1. Lin Tran _____ from _____.

2. Alex Marenko _____ from _____.

3. Ahmed Afar _____ from _____.

4. Marie Joseph _____ from _____.

5. I _____ from _____.

6 **Listen** Listen to the letters of the alphabet. Point to each letter as you hear it. Listen again and repeat each letter.

Aa	Bb	Cc	Dd	Ee	Ff	Gg	Hh	Ii	Jj	Kk	Ll	Mm
Nn	Oo	Pp	Qq	Rr	Ss	Tt	Uu	Vv	Ww	Xx	Yy	Zz

7 **Group Practice** Work in a large group. Sit in a circle. Each student says one letter of the alphabet. The next person in the circle says the next letter. Continue until your group says every letter of the alphabet.

8 **Say It** Practice the conversation with a partner.

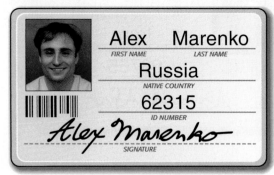

A: Good morning. What's your name?

B: My name is <u>Alex Marenko.</u>

A: Please spell your last name.

B: <u>M-A-R-E-N-K-O</u>.

Fill in the ID card below with your own information. Then practice the conversation again with the information from your ID card.

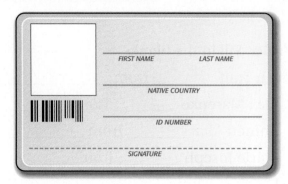

9 **Listen** Listen for the correct letters. Complete the names.

1. An_el_ Dom_ng_ 2. _le_ Ma_e_ _o 3. _o_a Lo_ez

> **Note:** Alphabetical order means *in the order of the alphabet.*
> **Example:** 1. <u>A</u>ngela
> 2. <u>B</u>ill
> 3. <u>C</u>arlos

10 **Write** Write the names in alphabetical order.

Lin <u>Alex</u>

Cindy _____

Marie _____

Alex _____

11 **Teamwork Task** Work in teams of five. Make a list of the first names of the students on your team. Then put the names in alphabetical order.

FIRST NAMES	FIRST NAMES IN ALPHABETICAL ORDER
1. _____	1. _____
2. _____	2. _____
3. _____	3. _____
4. _____	4. _____
5. _____	5. _____

Homework

Make a list of the people you live or work with. Write their first names in alphabetical order.

Game Time

Write a different letter of the alphabet in each of the boxes below. When your teacher says one of your letters, cross out that letter. When all your letters are crossed out, say "BINGO!"

Introducing My Family

Angela's Family Tree

Anna

Ramon
father

Rosa

Tomas

Angela

Hector

Juan

Gloria

① **Listen** Listen and write one of these words under each person in the picture: *son, daughter, father, mother, sister, brother, husband, wife, parents, children.*

> **Note:** Use *'s* after a name or noun to show possession.
> Hector**'s** brother = His brother   My sister**'s** family = Her family

② **Pair Practice** Practice the questions and answers with a partner.

1. Who is Ramon?   <u>He</u>   is Angela's   <u>father</u>   .
2. Who is Hector?   _____ is Angela's   _____ .
3. Who is Gloria?   _____ is Angela's   _____ .
4. Who are Juan and Gloria?   _____ are Angela's   _____ .
5. Who are Ramon and Anna?   _____ are Angela's   _____ .
6. Who is Angela's son?   _____ is Angela's son.
7. Who is Angela's sister?   _____ is Angela's sister.
8. Who is Angela's brother?   _____ is Angela's brother.

3 **Say It** Practice the conversation with two classmates.

husband

A: This is my <u>husband</u>, <u>Hector</u>.
B: Hello, <u>Hector</u>. Nice to meet you.
C: Nice to meet you, too.

Practice the conversation again with your classmates. This time use the pictures below.

1. daughter

2. friend

3. brother

Culture Tip

Introductions

For informal introductions, use only the first name.

Example: *This is my friend, Dimitri.*

For more formal introductions, or business introductions, use first and last names or titles.

Example: *This is my teacher, Eric Ryan.*

4 **Group Practice** Work in groups of four or five. Introduce one of your classmates to another classmate.

Example: *Student 1:* This is my classmate. His/Her name is _____.
Student 2: Hello _____ . Nice to meet you.

5 **Pair Practice** Show photographs of your family members or friends to your partner. Tell your partner about the people in the pictures.

Example: She is my sister. Her name is Lola.

single   married   divorced

Culture Tip

Wedding Rings

In the U.S. married people usually wear a wedding ring on the fourth finger of their left hand. Where do people wear wedding rings in your country?

6 **Say It** Practice the conversations with a partner.

A: Is <u>Angela</u> married?
B: Yes, <u>she</u> is.

A: Is <u>Lin</u> married?
B: No, <u>she's</u> single.

Angela   Lin

Practice the conversations again. This time use the pictures below.

Hector   Marie   Cindy

GRAMMAR CHECK

be: Contractions

Full Form	Contraction	Example Sentences
I am	**I'm**	**I'm** a student.
you are	**you're**	**You're** from Brazil.
he is	**he's**	**He's** my husband.
she is	**she's**	**She's** my mother.
it is	**it's**	**It's** my phone number.
we are	**we're**	**We're** brothers.
they are	**they're**	**They're** my parents.

Check Point:

✓ Use contractions for questions, too:

What is = **What's**   **What's** your name?

Who is = **Who's**   **Who's** he?

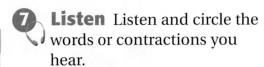

7 **Listen** Listen and circle the words or contractions you hear.

1. (She is /(She's)) my mother.

2. (What is / What's) your name?

3. (You are / You're) my friend.

4. (They are / They're) from Japan.

5. (It is / It's) a pencil.

6. (We are / We're) students.

7. (I am / I'm) Chiara.

8. (He is / He's) my son.

8 **Write** Write each sentence using contractions.

1. She is my friend.   <u>She's my friend</u>   .

2. He is my brother.   _____ .

3. They are my parents.   _____ .

4. We are a family.   _____ .

5. You are a student.   _____ .

6. I am a mother.   _____ .

9 **Teamwork Task** Work in teams of 3 or 4. Choose one student volunteer. On a piece of paper, draw a family tree for the student volunteer. Ask the volunteer questions to fill in the family tree. Ask about wife/husband, parents, children, brothers, and sisters. Write their names in the family tree. Then write sentences about the people in the volunteer's family.

Example: Linda is Albert's wife.

Game Time

Your teacher will write the name of someone in his/her family on the board. Ask questions to find out who the person is.

Example: Is she your wife?
Is she your mother?

What's Your Number?

1 **Listen** Listen and repeat the numbers.

0	1	2	3	4	5	6	7	8	9	10
zero	one	two	three	four	five	six	seven	eight	nine	ten

11	12	13	14	15	16	17	18	19
eleven	twelve	thirteen	fourteen	fifteen	sixteen	seventeen	eighteen	nineteen

20	30	40	50	60	70	80	90	100
twenty	thirty	forty	fifty	sixty	seventy	eighty	ninety	one hundred

2 **Pair Practice** Point to numbers in the box. Your partner will say the numbers. Check your partner's pronunciation. Then your partner points and you say the numbers.

3 **Say It** Practice the conversation with a partner.

A: I need information for your job application form.

B: OK.

A: What is your address?

B: It's <u>235 Apple Street</u>.

A: And your city and state?

B: <u>Santa Monica, California</u>.

A: And what's your zip code?

B: It's <u>90405</u>.

Practice the conversation again. This time use the applications below.

JOB APPLICATION
PERSONAL INFORMATION
PLEASE PRINT
Name _Nina Smith_
Street Address _229 Patriot Ave._
City _Boston_
State _Massachusetts_ Zip Code _02129_

JOB APPLICATION
PERSONAL INFORMATION
PLEASE PRINT
Name _Brian Clark_
Street Address _45 Winter Place_
City _Chicago_
State _Illinois_ Zip Code _60614_

4 Listen Listen to the addresses. Write the missing numbers.

1. __ __ Clark Street

2. __ __ __ Brown Street

3. __ __ East End Avenue

4. Apartment __ __

5. __ __ __ River Street

6. __ __ __ Avenue A

5 Say It Practice the conversation with a partner.

A: What's your telephone number?

B: It's <u>555-3412</u>.

A: I'm sorry. Could you repeat that?

B: Yes. <u>555-3412</u>.

A: And your area code?

B: (<u>818</u>).

Practice the conversation again. This time use the applications below.

6 Group Practice Work in groups of three. Ask the other students in your group their phone numbers. (You can give your real telephone number or make up a telephone number.) Write each person's name and telephone number below.

Name _____

Phone number

_____

Name _____

Phone number

_____

Name _____

Phone number

_____

Possessive Adjectives

Pronoun	Possessive Adjective	Example Sentences
I	**my**	**My** name is Eric.
you	**your**	**Your** area code is (212).
he	**his**	**His** teacher is American.
she	**her**	**Her** brother is a student.
it	**its**	**Its** tail is black.
we	**our**	**Our** native country is Brazil.
they	**their**	**Their** house is in San Francisco.

7 **Write** Write the correct possessive adjectives.

1. You are Laura.   _____ name is Laura.

2. She is from Mexico.   _____ native country is Mexico.

3. We live in Seattle.   _____ city is Seattle.

4. They live in Apartment 12.   _____ apartment number is 12.

5. I live in Texas.   _____ state is Texas.

8 **Say It** Practice the conversation with a partner.

A: What's <u>his</u> address?

B: <u>His</u> address is <u>454 Capital Street</u>.

A: And what's <u>his</u> city and state?

B: <u>Tallahassee, Florida</u>.

A: What's <u>his</u> telephone number?

B: <u>His</u> telephone number is <u>(850) 555-9328</u>.

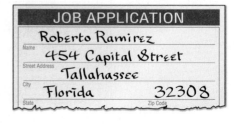

Fill in the application with your own information. Then practice the conversation again. This time use the information from your job application.

Titles

In formal situations, use one of these titles before a person's name:

Mr. = A man (*Mr.* is pronounced *mister.*)

Ms. = A woman (*Ms.* is pronounced *miz.*)

Miss = A single woman (*Miss* is pronounced *miss.*)

Mrs. = A married woman (*Mrs.* is pronounced *missuz*)

THE BIG DEAL DEPT. STORE

EMPLOYEE DIRECTORY

NAME	ADDRESS	PHONE NUMBER
Miss Maria Calvo	124 Center Street, Pasadena, CA	(626) 555-7746
Mr. Richard Klein	75 Third Avenue, Apt. 1A, Los Angeles, CA	(213) 555 - 3277
Mr. James Miller	36 North Street, Apt. 3B, Venice, CA	(310) 555-0457
Mrs. Mary Lynn Pitt	100 Park Avenue, Canoga Park, CA	(818) 555-1369
Ms. Reiko Yoda	54 Front Street, Manhattan Beach, CA	(323) 555-4476

9 **Write** Use the employee directory to answer the questions.

1. What is Mr. Miller's area code? <u>His area code is (310)</u>   .

2. What is Miss Calvo's address? _____ .

3. What is Mr. Klein's telephone number? _____ .

4. What is Mrs. Pitt's city? _____ .

5. What is Ms. Yoda's area code? _____ .

6. What is Mr. Miller's address? _____ .

10 **Pair Practice** Work with a partner. Ask and answer the questions in Exercise 9. Then ask and answer more questions about the employee directory.

11 **Listen** Listen and write the missing letters and numbers on the envelope.

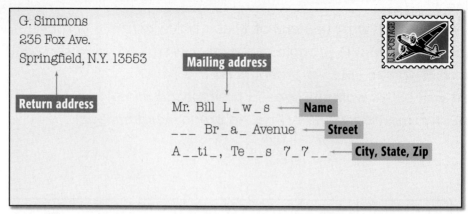

12 **Pair Practice** Work with a partner. Ask your partner his/her name, street, city, state, and zip code. Fill in the mailing address with the information your partner gives you. Then put your return address at the top. You can use your real address, or you can make up an address. Then exchange books with a partner to check your partner's work.

Game Time

Write a number from one to twenty in each box below. When your teacher says one of the numbers, cross the number out. When all of your numbers are crossed out, say "BINGO!"

1 **Listen and Read** Listen to the story. Then read the story.

My Family

My name is Angela Domingo. I'm married. My husband's name is Hector. We're from Mexico, but Los Angeles, California, is our home now.

Our son, Juan, is eight years old. Gloria is our daughter. She's six. Our address is 215 West Second Street. Our telephone number is (818) 555-3412.

My sister is in Los Angeles, too. Her name is Rosa Lopez. She's single. My brother is here, too. His name is Tomas. He's divorced. My family is happy in Los Angeles.

2 **Read** Read the sentences. Circle *True* or *False*.

1. Hector is Angela's husband.	True	False
2. Gloria is 8 years old.	True	False
3. Angela's area code is (518).	True	False
4. Rosa Lopez is Angela's mother.	True	False
5. Rosa is married.	True	False
6. Angela's brother is divorced.	True	False

3 **Write** Write about *your* family. Follow Angela's example.

My name is _____ . I am _____ .

I am from _____ but _____ my home now.

4 **Best Answer** Bubble the correct answer.   **a**   **b**

1. Where are you from?
   a) Fine, thank you.   **b)** Mexico.   ○   ●

2. Are you married?
   a) Yes, I are married.   **b)** Yes, I am married.   ○   ○

3. Please spell your name.
   a) L-I-N.   **b)** Thank you.   ○   ○

4. Who is he?
   a) He's my brother.   **b)** He is my daughter.   ○   ○

5. What's your area code?
   a) 555-3454.   **b)** It's (310).   ○   ○

5 **Write** Write the words for the numbered items in the picture.

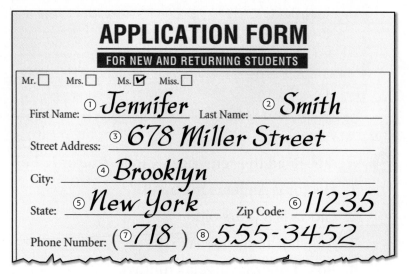

1. <u>first name</u>
2. _____
3. _____
4. _____
5. _____
6. _____
7. _____
8. _____

6 **Pair Practice** Read the information. Work with a partner to address the envelope from Lin Tran to her friend.

> Hello. My name is Lin Tran. I live at 229 Park Avenue. I live in Los Angeles, California. My zip code is 91303. I am writing to my friend. His first name is Michael. His last name is Lawson. He lives in Miami, Florida. His address is 141 Grove Street. His zip code is 33176.

U.S. POSTAGE

_____
_____
_____
_____

_____
_____
_____

7 **Write** Write your personal information in the student registration form.

APPLICATION FORM
FOR NEW AND RETURNING STUDENTS

Mr. ☐   Mrs. ☐   Ms. ☐   Miss. ☐

First Name: _____   Last Name: _____

Street Address: _____

City: _____   State: _____

Zip Code: _____   Phone Number: (___) _____

Signature: _____

INTERNET IDEA
Search the Internet for information about your name. Use one or more of these search words: *name, meaning, origin.* What does your name mean? What country/culture is it from? Tell your class about your name.

Pronunciation Short *i* and long *e*

A. Listen to the word pairs. The first word has the short *i* sound (/i/ as in *it*). The second word has the long *e* sound (/e/ as in *eat*).

1. (is)	ease	5. fill	feel
2. hit	heat	6. sick	seek
3. its	eats	7. itch	each
4. sit	seat	8. live	leave

B. Listen and circle the word you hear.

8 Teamwork Task Work with a large group to create a directory of names, addresses, and telephone numbers of all the students on your team.

A. Each person writes their first and last name on an index card.

B. The group works together to alphabetize the cards by last names.

C. Make a directory of your group on a sheet of paper. Write the list in alphabetical order. Make sure the directory has all of this information:

Name	Address	TELEPHONE
Alvarez, Manuel	45 Avenue Z	(718) 555-9436
	Bronx, New York 10457	

D. You can make a copy of the directory for everyone on your team.

I can . . .			
spell my name.	1	2	3
greet people.	1	2	3
introduce myself and others.	1	2	3
identify family members.	1	2	3
say my address and phone number.	1	2	3
fill out an application form.	1	2	3
address an envelope.	1	2	3
use the alphabet and numbers.	1	2	3
alphabetize names.	1	2	3
make statements with be.	1	2	3
use possessive adjectives.	1	2	3

1 = not well   2 = OK   3 = very well

9 **Write** Write the missing words in the cartoon story. Use these words: *meet, are, My, Her, She's, from, I'm, they, single, parents.*

Alberto: Good Morning. (1) _____ name is Alberto.
Rosa: Hi. (2) _____ Rosa.

Alberto: Nice to (3)____ you, Rosa.
Rosa: Nice to meet you, too.

Alberto: And who (4) _____ you?
Rosa: (5) _____ my very good friend.
(6)_____ name is Cindy.

Alberto: Where are you (7) _____, Cindy?
Cindy: Right here in Los Angeles. I'm a native Californian.

Alberto: How about your (8) _____?
Are they from L.A. too?
Cindy: Yes, (9) _____ are.

Alberto: And your . . . husband? Are you married, Cindy?
Cindy: No, Alberto, I'm (10) _____. How about you?

10 **Group Practice** Work in groups of three. Practice the story.

School

GOALS

✓ Name classroom objects
✓ Identify school places
✓ Identify school jobs
✓ Ask for and tell locations
✓ Give and follow instructions
✓ Use *a* and *an*
✓ Understand singular and plural nouns
✓ Ask questions with *be*

Eric

Frank

Lara

3.75

22

CHAPTER 2

Listen

Listen and point to the words you hear. Then point to each item in the picture. Listen again and repeat each word.

1. teacher
2. student
3. desk
4. chair
5. apple
6. notebook
7. pencil
8. eraser
9. board
10. map
11. classroom
12. counselor
13. pen
14. umbrella
15. office assistant
16. folder
17. office
18. cook
19. cashier
20. cafeteria
21. librarian
22. book
23. computer
24. library

23

1 **Pair Practice** Work with a partner. Point to things in the picture on pages 22–23. Ask: *What's this?* Your partner says what the things are. Take turns.

Example: *Student 1:* What's this?
Student 2: It's a desk.

GRAMMAR CHECK

a/an	
a	*an*
a pen	**an** apple
a library	**an** office

Check Points:
✓ Use **a** and **an** with singular nouns.
✓ Use **an** before nouns that begin with *a, e, i, o,* or *u.*

2 **Write** Write the word for each thing. Write *a* or *an* before each word.

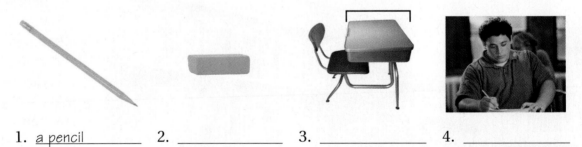

1. <u>a pencil</u>　　2. _____　　3. _____　　4. _____

5. _____　　6. _____　　7. _____　　8. _____

3 **Say It** Practice the conversations with a partner.

A: What's this?
B: It's <u>a</u> <u>pen</u>.

pen

A: What's that?
B: It's <u>an</u> <u>apple</u>.

apple

Practice the conversations again. This time use the pictures below.

1. **notebook**

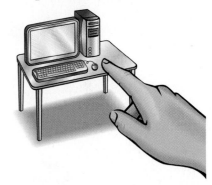

2. **computer**

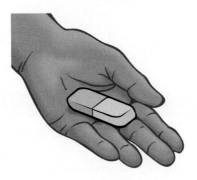

3. **eraser**

4. **map**

4 **Pair Practice** Work with a partner. Ask and answer questions about things in your classroom. Use *this* and *that*.

Example: *Student 1:* What's that?
Student 2: It's a clock.

Note Use *they* to talk about two or more things.

5 **Say It** Practice the conversation with a partner.

A: What's this?

B: It's a <u>notebook</u>.

A: What are they?

B: They are <u>notebooks</u>.

Practice the conversation again. This time use the pictures below.

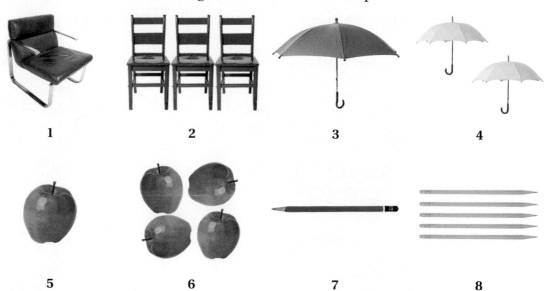

1   2   3   4

5   6   7   8

GRAMMAR CHECK

Singular and plural			
		Example Sentences	
Singular	*Plural*	*Singular*	*Plural*
pen	pens	It is a **pen**.	They are **pens**.
book	books	It is a **book**.	They are **books**.
student	students	He is a **student**.	We are **students**.

Check Points:
- ✓ *Singular* means *one*. *Plural* means *more than one*.
- ✓ Add *s* to the end of most nouns to make them plural.
- ✓ Use *is* with singular nouns. Use *are* with plural nouns.

6 Write Write the word for each object or person. Write *a* or *an* before singular nouns. Add *s* to the word for plural nouns.

1. an apple _____   2. _____   3. _____

4. _____   5. _____   6. _____

7 Group Practice Work in groups of six to eight students. Stand in a line. The first student in line identifies an object in the classroom. The next student says that object and adds another. Continue until the last student speaks. Remember to use *this* when an object is close to you, *that* when it is not, and *they* for more than one object.

Example: *Student 1:* This is an eraser.
   Student 2: That is an eraser and that is a clock.
   Student 3: That's an eraser and that's a clock and they are chairs.

8 Teamwork Task Work in teams of four. Look around your classroom. On a piece of paper, list as many objects in your classroom as you can.

Students 1 and 2: list singular objects. (a board)

Students 3 and 4: list plural objects. (chairs)

Homework

How many objects in your classroom do you also have at home? Make a list. Remember to use *a* or *an* when you only have one, and use the plural *s* when you have more than one.

Locations and Directions

GRAMMAR CHECK

Prepositions

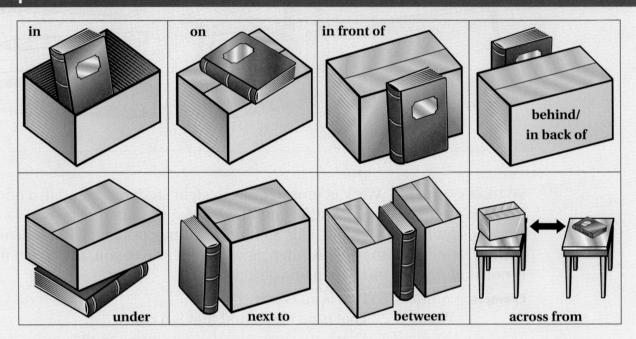

| in | on | in front of | behind/ in back of |
| under | next to | between | across from |

1 **Pair Practice** Work with a partner. Point to one of the pictures of the book and the box. Ask: *Where is the book?* Your partner answers. Take turns.

Example: *Student 1:* Where is the book?
Student 2: The book is in the box.

2 **Group Practice** Work in groups of three or four. Look at the picture on pages 22–23. With your group, write sentences with prepositions about the people and places at the school. Write as many sentences as you can.

Example: Peter is behind the desk.

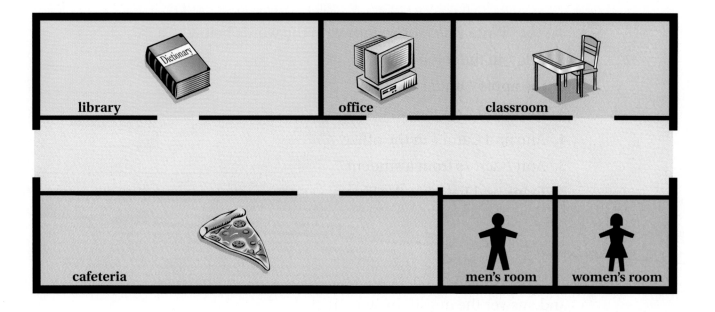

library office classroom

cafeteria men's room women's room

3 **Pair Practice** Look at the map of the school. With your partner, ask and answer the questions below.

Example: *Student 1:* Is the office next to the cafeteria?
     Student 2: Yes, it is. (*or* No, it isn't.)

1. Is the library across from the cafeteria? _____

2. Is the library between the office and the men's room? _____

3. Is the cafeteria next to the men's room? _____

4. Is the classroom next to the office? _____

5. Is the cafeteria between the office and the women's room? _____

6. Is the office across from the women's room? _____

GRAMMAR CHECK

Be: Yes/No questions and short answers

Yes/No questions			Short answers	
Be	**Subject**		**Yes**	**No**
Am	I	in Room 303?	Yes, you are.	No, you aren't.
Is	he/she/it	behind Maria?	Yes, he/she/it is.	No, he/she/it isn't.
Are	you	behind me?	Yes, I am.	No, I'm not.
Are	you/we/they	next to the office?	Yes, you/we/they are.	No, you/we/they aren't.

Check Points:

✓ Use contractions for negative short answers. Do not use contractions for short answers with *yes*.

✓ Other negative contractions include *you're not, he's not, she's not, it's not, we're not, they're not.*

4 Write Write *yes/no* questions with the words below.

1. Eric / in the classroom   <u>Is Eric in the classroom</u>   ?
2. the apple / under the desk   _____ ?
3. the board / on the wall   _____ ?
4. Ann and Carol / in the office   _____ ?
5. Ann / across from a student   _____ ?
6. Frank and Lara / in the library   _____ ?

5 Pair Practice Look at the picture on pages 22–23. With a partner, ask and answer the questions in Activity 4.

6 Say It Practice the conversation with a partner.

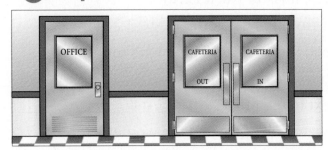

A: Excuse me. Where is <u>the office</u>?
B: It's <u>next to the cafeteria</u>.
A: Thank you.
B: You're welcome.

The office?

Practice the conversation again. This time use the pictures below.

1. The cafeteria?   2. The men's room?   3. The library?

7 Write Write about your school.

1. Where is your classroom?   My classroom is _____.
2. Where is the cafeteria?   _____.
3. Where are the bathrooms?   _____.
4. Where is the office?   _____.
5. Where is the library?   _____.

GRAMMAR CHECK

Be: Wh- questions

Wh- word	be	Subject
Where	am	I?
Where	is	he/she/it?
Where	are	we/they?
Who	am	I?
Who	is	he/she/it?
Who	are	we/they?

Check Points:
- ✓ You can add a preposition between *Who is/are* and the subject: *Who is next to her?*
- ✓ Other *wh-* question words are *when, what, why*, and *how*.

8 Pair Practice Work with a partner. Student 1 uses Seating Chart A on this page. Student 2 uses Seating Chart B on page 32. Ask and answer *who* questions with *next to, between, in front of,* and *behind* to complete the chart. Start with questions about Angela.

Example: *Student 1:* Who is in front of Angela?
   Student 2: Lin is in front of Angela.

Seating Chart: A
Teacher (Front)

Marie		Sonia	
	Angela		Sarah
		Yakov	
Ella	José		Ahmed

(Back)

Seating Chart: B
Teacher (Front)

	Lin		Carmen
Alex	Angela	George	
Henri	Fatima		Andrea
		Igor	

(Back)

9 **Write** Answer the questions about the completed seating chart.

1. Who is behind Marie? _____ .
2. Who is next to Sarah? _____ .
3. Who is between Fatima and Andrea? _____ .
4. Who is in front of Sarah? _____ .
5. Where is Henri? _____ .
6. Where is Lin? _____ .
7. Where is Alex? _____ .
8. Where is George? _____ .

10 **Teamwork Task** Work in teams of three or four. Create a seating chart for your class. Then write sentences about the students in your class. Write as many as you can. Use as many different prepositions as you can.

Example: 1: Rosa is next to Ali.
2: Ali is behind Ana.

Game Time

Work in teams. Your teacher will write the name of a student on a piece of paper. Try to guess who the student is by asking yes/no questions with prepositions. (Example: *Is he next to Berta?*) Each team gets a point for every right guess.

School Jobs

1 **Say It** Practice the conversation with a partner.

A: Is <u>Freddy</u> a <u>teacher</u>?

B: No, <u>he</u> isn't. <u>He</u>'s a <u>cook</u>.

Freddy / teacher? / cook

Practice the conversation again. This time use the pictures below.

1. **Eric / student? / teacher**   2. **Ann / cashier? / counselor**   3. **Robin / cook? / cashier**

2 **Write** Write *yes/no* questions with the words below.

1. Freddy / office assistant?   <u>Is Freddy an office assistant</u> ?

2. Robin / cashier?   _____ ?

3. Carol / office assistant?   _____ ?

4. Peter / counselor?   _____ ?

5. Eric / cook?   _____ ?

6. Ann / librarian?   _____ ?

3 Pair Practice Look at the workers in the school on pages 22–23. With a partner, ask and answer questions about the workers.

Example: *Student 1:* Is Frank an office assistant?
Student 2: No, he isn't. He's a cook.

4 Write Look at the school on pages 22–23. Write the answers.

1. Where is the office assistant?   1. <u>She is in the office</u> .
2. Where is the student?   2. _____ .
3. Where is the librarian?   3. _____ .
4. Where is the teacher?   4. _____ .
5. Where are the cook and the cashier? 5. _____ .

5 Pair Practice Work with a partner. Ask and answer *who* and *where* questions about the workers in the school on pages 22–23.

Example: *Student 1:* Who is Eric?
Student 2: He is a teacher.
Student 1: Where is he?
Student 2: He is in the classroom.

Culture Tip

Teacher's Names
Some teachers in the U.S. are informal and want students to use their first names. Other teachers are more formal and want students to use their last names. What name does your teacher prefer?

6 Listen Listen and circle the worker you hear.

1. teacher / cook   4. cashier / librarian
2. cook / cashier   5. office assistant / teacher
3. counselor / office assistant   6. cook / librarian

7 **Say It** Practice the conversation with a partner.

A: Please, <u>arrive on time</u>.
B: <u>Arrive on time</u>?
A: Yes, please.
B: OK.
A: Thank you.

arrive on time

Practice the conversation again. This time use the pictures below.

1. **bring more water**

2. **return the book next week**

3. **help the customer**

GRAMMAR CHECK

Imperatives	
Positive	*Negative*
Open your books.	**Don't open** your books.
Put the pencils on the desk.	**Don't put** the pencils on the desk.

Check Point:
✓ Polite imperative: **Please open** your books.

Culture Tip

Arrive on time
Company managers in the United States expect their workers to be on time every day. Don't arrive late!

8 **Say It** Practice the conversation with a partner.

A: Please don't <u>eat in the office</u>.
B: I'm sorry. Could you repeat that?
A: Yes. Don't <u>eat in the office</u>.
B: Oh, OK. Sorry.

eat in the office

Practice the conversation again. This time use the pictures below.

1. smoke in the cafeteria

2. park here

3. talk in the library

9 **Teamwork Task** Work in teams of three or four. Make a list of different jobs at your school. Write the places where they work.

JOB	PLACE
teacher	classroom

Game Time

Where are the keys?
Try to find your teachers keys. They are somewhere in the classroom. Ask "Yes/No" questions to find them.
Example: "Are they in your pocket?" "No, they aren't."

1 **Listen and Read** Listen to the story. Then read the story.

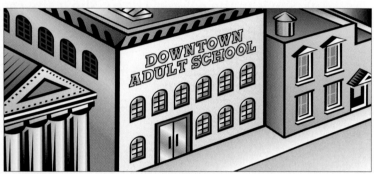

My School

Hi. I'm Angela. I'm a student at the Downtown Adult School. My sister is a student, too, but she isn't in my class. Her class is in Room 25. I'm in Room 33. Room 33 is next to the library and across from the office. I'm in class right now. Lin Tran is in front of me and Marie is behind me. They are both good friends. George Chung is between me and his wife. He isn't in class every day, but he's a good student. All the students in my class are nice people.

The staff at my school is great. Mr. Ryan is my teacher. He's a really good teacher. Carol is the office assistant. She's a hard worker, and she's very friendly. Ann Page is the counselor. Go to her if you have a problem. I'm very happy at the Downtown Adult School because all the people are so helpful and nice.

2 **Write** Answer the questions about the story.

1. Is Angela at home now? _____.

2. Is Mr. Ryan Angela's teacher? _____.

3. Is George Chung a good student? _____.

4. Is Lin Tran behind Angela? _____.

5. Who is Ann Page? _____.

6. Who is Carol? _____.

7. Where is Marie? _____.

8. Where is Angela's class? _____.

3 **Write** On a piece of paper, write about *your* school. What is the name of your school? What room are you in? Who is your teacher? Who is next to you?

④ Best Answer Bubble the correct answer.

                                                       a   **b**

1. What's that?
   a) It's an computer.   b) It's an eraser.   ○   ●

2. Are you a student?
   a) Yes, I am.   b) Yes, I'm.   ○   ○

3. Who is she?
   a) She is in the cafeteria.   b) She is the cashier.   ○   ○

4. Where is the class?
   a) It's next to the office.   b) Yes, it is.   ○   ○

5. Please open your book.
   a) Thank you.   b) OK.   ○   ○

⑤ Write Write the words for the numbered items in the picture.

1. <u>student</u>

2. _____

3. _____

4. _____

5. _____

6. _____

7. _____

8. _____

9. _____

6 **Problem Solving** What's wrong with this classroom? Write one sentence about each thing in the wrong place. Use prepositions in your sentences.

1. <u>The chair is on the desk</u>   .

2. _____.

3. _____.

4. _____.

5. _____.

7 **Pair Practice** Work with your partner to write instructions for fixing the classroom. Use imperatives.

1. <u>Put the chair behind the desk</u>   .

2. _____.

3. _____.

4. _____.

5. _____.

INTERNET IDEA

Search the Internet for information about your school or a school you would like to go to. Where is the school? What can you study at the school? How many students are there at the school? Tell your class about the school.

Pronunciation a and an

A. We usually pronounce the word *a* like "uh." Listen and repeat.

a pen   a teacher
a box   a good student
a cook

B. We pronounce the "a" in *an* with a short *a* sound. Listen and repeat.

an apple   an office
an eraser   an adult
an umbrella

8 Teamwork Task

A. Work in small teams. Pretend there is a new student in class. Make a list of class and school instructions for the student. Write as many instructions about your class and school as you can. Write the instructions in imperative sentences.

B. Use poster paper to make posters of the instructions. Put all of the positive instructions on one poster. Put all the negative instructions on another poster. Draw pictures next to some of the instructions.

C. Hang your posters up in class.

Example:

YES	NO
Speak English in class.	Don't write in school books.

I can...			
• name classroom objects.	1	2	3
• identify school places.	1	2	3
• identify school jobs.	1	2	3
• ask for and tell locations.	1	2	3
• give and follow instructions.	1	2	3
• use *a* and *an*.	1	2	3
• understand singular and plural nouns.	1	2	3
• ask questions with *be*.	1	2	3

1 = not well   2 = OK   3 = very well

Cindy: Excuse me. where is Room 103? Is it (1)_____ to the office?

Woman: No, it (2)_____ . It's (3)_____ from the office. It's (4)_____ the cafeteria and the library.
Cindy: Thank you.

Cindy: Is (5)_____ Room 103?
Teacher: Yes, (6)_____ is. Please (7)_____ in.

Teacher: Please, (8)_____ your books and (9)_____ page 85.

Teacher: Please sit down. There is a seat right (10)_____ Alberto.
Cindy: Alberto?

Alberto: Cindy!!!

⑩ **Group Practice** Work in groups of four. Practice the story.

Shopping

T
DEPA

42

Listen

Listen and point to the words you hear. Then point to each item in the picture. Listen again and repeat each word.

1. cashier
2. customer
3. check
4. receipt
5. bills
6. change
7. dress
8. blouse
9. sweater
10. skirt
11. belt
12. jacket
13. shirt
14. pants
15. shoes
16. suit
17. tie
18. salesperson
19. white
20. yellow
21. gray
22. green
23. red
24. orange
25. brown
26. blue
27. black

1 **Say It** Practice the conversation with a partner.

A: What color <u>shoes</u> do you like?

B: I like <u>black</u> <u>shoes</u>. How about you?

A: I like <u>brown</u> <u>shoes</u>.

shoes

Practice the conversation again. This time use the pictures below.

1. shorts

2. T-shirts

3. sweaters

GRAMMAR CHECK

Simple present		
Subject	*Verb*	
I/You/We/They	**need** **like** **want** **have**	black shoes.
He/She/It	**needs** **likes** **wants** **has**	a red shirt.

2 **Pair Practice** Work with a partner. Ask your partner what color clothes he or she likes. Then write the color next to the clothes.

Example: *Student 1:* What color shoes do you like?

Student 2: I like brown shoes.

1. <u>brown</u> shoes
2. _____ shirts
3. _____ jackets
4. _____ shorts
5. _____ pants
6. _____ sweaters

3 **Write** Write sentences about clothes your partner likes. Use the information from Activity 2.

1. <u>Marco likes brown shoes</u>   .
2. _____ .
3. _____ .
4. _____ .
5. _____ .
6. _____ .

Tell the class what color clothes your partner likes.

4 **Group Practice** Work in groups of five or six. Stand in a line. The first student in line tells what kind of clothes he or she likes to wear. The next student tells what the first student likes to wear and adds what he or she likes to wear. Continue until the last student speaks.

Example: *Student 1:* I like black shoes.
                     Student 2: Marco likes black shoes and I like blue jeans.

5 **Say It** Practice the conversation with a partner.

blue jacket?

A: Do you want a <u>jacket</u>?

B: Yes, I do.

A: Do you want a <u>blue jacket</u>?

B: No, I don't. I want a <u>black jacket</u>.

A: Here is a nice <u>black jacket</u>.

Practice the conversation again. This time use the pictures below.

1. **yellow sweater?**

2. **brown suit?**

3. **yellow tie?**

Simple present *yes/no* questions and short answers

Do/Does	Subject	Verb		Short Answers	
				Yes	**No**
Do	I/you/we/they	**like**	jeans?	**Yes,** I/you/ we/they **do.**	**No,** I/you/ we/they **don't.**
Does	he/she/it	**want**	a suit?	**Yes,** he/she/ it **does.**	**No,** he/she/ it **doesn't.**

6 **Pair Practice** Work with a partner. Ask what kind of clothes he or she has. Put a check under *Yes* or *No*.

Example: *Student 1:* Do you have a blue suit?
Student 2: Yes, I do.

FOR A MAN	YES	NO	FOR A WOMAN	YES	NO
a blue suit?	√		a red dress?		
a white shirt?			a green blouse?		
black pants?			a yellow skirt?		
a brown jacket?			a white jacket?		
orange shoes?			black shoes?		

Tell the class what color clothes your partner has.

7 **Pair Practice** Ask and answer questions about Hector and Angela's clothes. Student 1 asks about Hector's clothes. Student 2 asks about Angela's.

Example: *Student 1:* Does Hector have a suit in his closet?
Student 2: Yes, he does.
Student 1: What color suit does he have?

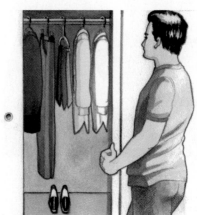

Simple present: *Wh-* questions

Wh- word	*do/does*	*Subject*	*Verb*
What	**do**	I/you/we/they	**want?**
What	**does**	he/she/it	**need?**

Check Points:

✓ You can add a noun between the *wh-* word and *do/does*:
  What **color** do you have?
  What **size** do you need?

✓ Other *wh-* question words are *who, when, where, why,* and *how.*

8 **Teamwork Task** Work in teams of three. Choose a volunteer for Student 1. Write his or her name in the box. Ask about his or her clothes.
Student 2 asks, "What clothes do you have in your closet?"
Student 3 asks, "What color _____s do you have?"

Name	Clothes	Colors
Maria	shirts	white, yellow
	pants	black, blue

Homework

Look in your closet at home. Write what clothes you have and the color of the clothes. Write ten things.

Money

Word Help: Money

penny

nickel

dime

quarter

one-dollar bill

five-dollar bill

ten-dollar bill

twenty-dollar bill

1 **Say It** Practice the conversation with a partner.

A: What's this?

B: It's a <u>quarter</u>.

A: How much is it worth?

B: <u>Twenty-five cents</u>.

Practice the conversation again. This time use the pictures below.

1

2

3

4

Note We write dollars and cents like this:

$ .30 (thirty cents) $2.00 (two dollars) $2.25 (two dollars and twenty-five cents)

2 Listen and Write Listen and write the price you hear.

1. _____   2. _____   3. _____   4. _____

3 Problem Solving Write the amount.

1. _____   2. _____   3. _____

> **Note** $5.95 = five dollars and ninety-five cents = five ninety-five
> $17.50 = seventeen dollars and fifty cents = seventeen fifty

4 Say It Practice the conversation with a partner.

A: How much money do you have?

B: I have <u>eighty-five cents</u>.

Practice the conversation again. This time use the amounts in Activity 3.

> **Note** Use *How much* like a *wh-* word:
> With *be*:   *How much is the pen? / How much are the pens?*
> With simple present: *How much do I have? / How much does he have?*

5 Write Fill in the blanks with *do*, *does*, *have*, or *has*.

1. How much _____ Hector have?   He _____ sixty-five cents.

2. How much _____ Lin have?   She _____ $12.50.

3. How much _____ you have?   I _____ $2.06.

4. How much _____ your teacher have?   He/She _____ forty dollars.

5. How much _____ Rosa and Cindy have?   They _____ a hundred dollars.

6 **Group Practice** Work in groups of four or five. Take out all the change (no bills!) from your pocket or purse. Ask the other students how much change they have. Use their answers to fill in the chart.

Name	How much does he/she have?
Masha	She has $1.25.

7 **Say It** Practice the conversation with a partner.

forty dollars

A: How much is the <u>shirt</u>?
B: It's <u>$29.95</u>.
A: How much does she have?
B: She has <u>forty</u> dollars.
A: She has enough.

Practice the conversation again. This time use the pictures below.

1. one hundred dollars

2. eighty dollars

3. twenty-five dollars

8 **Pair Practice** Work with a partner. Ask and answer questions about the prices of the clothes in the store window. Does Alex have enough for each item? Does he need more money?

9 **Pair Practice** Work with a partner. Ask and answer the questions about the receipt.

1. What is the name of the business? _____

2. What is the receipt for? _____

3. How much is the student book? How much are the workbooks? The dictionary? _____

4. What is the total? _____

⑩ Pair Practice Work with a partner. Ask and answer the questions about the check.

1. What is the date of the check? _____
2. How much is the check for? _____
3. Who is the check to? _____
4. What is the check for? _____

⑪ Write Write a check to the Bargain Books store for the total price on the receipt. Use the information in the receipt and your own name.

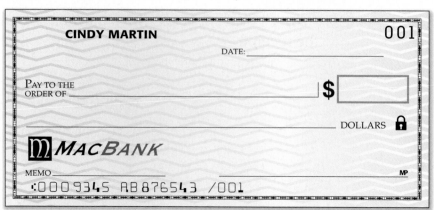

Game Time

Your teacher will show you an advertisement from a newspaper or catalog for an item of clothing on sale but will cover up the price. Guess how much the item costs.

Clothes for Work

Word Help: Sizes

small   medium   large   extra large

1 Say It Practice the conversation with a partner.

jacket

A: May I help you?

B: Yes, please. I'm looking for a <u>jacket</u> for work.

A: What size do you need?

B: I need a <u>medium</u>.

A: What color do you want?

B: <u>Blue</u>, please.

Practice the conversation again. This time use the pictures below.

1. blouse   2. sweater   3. dress

2 Listen and Write Listen to the conversations. Write the kind of clothes, colors, and sizes the people want.

	CLOTHES	COLOR	SIZE
1.	_____	_____	_____
2.	_____	_____	_____
3.	_____	_____	_____
4.	_____	_____	_____

Word Help: Shoes

high heel shoes

sandals

dress shoes

sneakers

boots

3 **Say It** Practice the conversation with a partner.

A: May I help you?

B: Yes, please. I need a pair of <u>dress shoes</u>.

A: OK. What color do you want?

B: Do you have <u>gray</u>?

A: Yes we do. What size do you need?

B: I need a size <u>8</u>.

A: Here you are — <u>gray</u>, <u>size 8 dress</u> shoes.

B: Great. Thank you very much.

Practice the conversation again. This time use the pictures below.

1

2

3

4 **Group Practice** Interview three classmates. Ask what kind of clothes and colors they have. Ask what kind of clothes and colors they want. Write their answers.

NAME	CLOTHES	COLOR
_____	_____	_____
_____	_____	_____
_____	_____	_____

5 **Say It** Practice the conversation with a partner.

A: Can I help you?

B: Yes, please. I need a brown dress.

A: I'm sorry. We don't have brown dresses. How about a black dress?

B: No, I don't need a black dress. Thanks anyway.

Practice the conversation again. This time use the pictures below.

1

3

2

Culture Tip

Polite language

Say **please** when you ask for something.

Say **sorry** when you say *no* to a request.

Say **thank you** when someone does something for you.

GRAMMAR CHECK

Simple present negative			
Subject	**do not (don't) / does not (doesn't)**	**Base verb**	
I/You/We/They	**do not (don't)**	have	red shoes.
He/She/It	**does not (doesn't)**	need	a size small.

6 **Write** Make the sentences negative. Use the words in parentheses.

1. Cindy needs black shoes. (red) _She doesn't need red shoes_ .

2. Lin wants a red dress. (orange) _____ .

3. Mr. Chung likes white pants. (green) _____ .

4. Elina has a black T-shirt. (pink) _____ .

5. Rosa likes black belts. (blue) _____ .

Clothes for work
Different kinds of clothes are good for different kinds of jobs. To find out what clothes are good for your job, ask your supervisor, or look around at the clothes your coworkers are wearing.

7 **Write** Make a list of clothes that are good to wear for your job (or the job you want) and clothes that are not good.

The job I have/want: _____

GOOD FOR MY JOB

_____

_____

_____

_____

NOT GOOD FOR MY JOB

_____

_____

_____

_____

8 **Teamwork Task** Work in groups of three or four. Look at Alex's closet. On a piece of paper, make a list of the clothes Alex has in his closet. Then make a list of the clothes in his closet that are good for his job. (Alex is a salesman.)

Homework
Interview two family members, friends, or neighbors about the clothes they wear for their job. Report back to the class about their work clothes.

1 Listen and Read Listen to the story. Then read the story.

Shopping for School

It is September and Angela's children need new clothes for school. Her son, Juan, needs a pair of pants. The department store has a pair of blue pants. Juan really likes them, but they are $50. He doesn't need *that* pair of pants!

Gloria is Angela's daughter. Gloria likes red clothes. She wants a red skirt, a red shirt, and red shoes. Does Gloria need red clothes? No, she doesn't. Gloria needs a uniform for school. The uniform is a black skirt, white shirt, and brown shoes. The skirt is $25, the shirt is $20, and the shoes are $40.

Angela is going to school, too. She is a student in an English class. Angela needs many things for her class. She needs a notebook, a dictionary, textbooks, and a good pen. Angela needs more money!

2 Write Read the sentences. Circle *True* or *False*.

1. Angela's children need new clothes for school.	True	False
2. Juan likes a pair of forty-dollar pants.	True	False
3. Gloria wants red clothes.	True	False
4. Gloria needs a uniform for school.	True	False
5. The skirt Gloria needs is $40.	True	False
6. Angela is a student in a math class.	True	False
7. Angela needs clothes for school.	True	False
8. Angela doesn't have enough money.	True	False

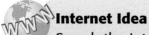
Internet Idea
Search the Internet for an item you want to buy. Use *shopping* as your search word. Also type in the kind of item you want (for example: *CD* or *clothes*). Where can you get the item? How much does it cost? How can you order it? Tell your class about the item.

3 **Best Answer** Bubble the correct answer.

                                                                             a   **b**

1. How much money does Angela have?
   a) She have $8.   b) She has $8.   ○   ●

2. What color ties do you like?
   a) I likes blue ties.   b) I like blue ties.   ○   ○

3. How much is the shirt?
   a) It's a large.   b) It's $25.50.   ○   ○

4. Do you have red shirts?
   a) No, we doesn't have red shirts.   b) No, we don't have red shirts.   ○   ○

5. Can I help you?
   a) I need a size small jacket.   b) I have enough money.   ○   ○

4 **Write** Write the words for the numbered items in the picture.

1. *customer*   7. _____

2. _____   8. _____

3. _____   9. _____

4. _____   10. _____

5. _____   11. _____

6. _____   12. _____

5 Listen
Listen to the conversation. Write the prices you hear on the right price tags.

Pronunciation /s/ and /z/

A. Listen for the /s/ sound at the end of each word. Repeat each word.

pants   socks   belts   checks   skirts

B. Listen for the /z/ sound at the end of each word. Repeat each word.

ties   customers   dollars   bills   shoes

C. Listen. Circle the words with the /s/ sound. Underline the words with the /z/ sound.

shirts   dimes   stores   jackets   suits

6 Teamwork Task

A. Work in teams of four or five. Pretend you are in a department store. Choose a student to be the salesperson. The other students are customers shopping together. Look at the clothes in the window. Each student tells the salesperson what he or she wants. Use the prompts below.

SALESPERSON		CUSTOMERS	
(Offer to help.)	*May . . .*	(Tell what you want.)	*I . . .*
(Ask about color.)	*What color . . .*	(Tell what color you want.)	*I . . .*
(Ask about size.)	*What size . . .*	(Tell what size you need.)	*I . . .*
(Give item to customer.)	*Here you are.*	(Ask the price.)	*How . . .*
(Tell the price.)	*It's . . .*	(Say if you want it.)	*I . . .*

B. Write a receipt from the department store for all of your team's clothing. Add up the cost. Write the total. See page 51 for an example of a receipt.

C. Write a check to the Big Deal Department Store for the total amount of the receipt. Sign the check with your name.

I can . . .			
• name clothes and colors.	1	2	3
• speak with salespeople.	1	2	3
• name and count money.	1	2	3
• talk about what I have, like, want, and need.	1	2	3
• talk about sizes.	1	2	3
• write a check.	1	2	3
• read a receipt.	1	2	3
• use the simple present tense.	1	2	3

1 = not well   2 = OK   3 = very well

Rosa: You have a date with Alberto. You (1)_____ something nice to wear.
Cindy: I need new pants and a new black (2)_____. Alberto (3)_____ black.

Rosa: What (4)_____ pants do you want?
Cindy: I (5)_____ blue, or maybe gray.

Rosa: What size do you (6)_____?
Cindy: Size 5, I think.

Rosa: Here is a size 5.
Cindy: How (7)_____ are they?
Rosa: $39.99.

Rosa: Do you have (8)_____?
Cindy: Yes. I (9)_____ $100.

Rosa: Great. Where are the nice (10)_____ jackets?

8 **Pair Practice** Practice the story with a partner.

Time

GOALS

- ✓ Ask for and tell the time
- ✓ Say and write times and dates
- ✓ Put dates in time order
- ✓ Say and write your date of birth
- ✓ Use ordinal numbers
- ✓ Talk about daily activities
- ✓ Read and understand an appointment card
- ✓ Read and understand a work schedule
- ✓ Use prepositions of time
- ✓ Understand simple present spelling changes with *he*, *she*, and *it*

	TUESDAY	WEDNESDAY	THURSDAY	FRIDAY	SATURDAY
2	3	4	5	6	7
9	10	11	12	13	14
16	17	18	19	20	21
23	24	25	26	27	28
30	31				

JULY 2007 ②

③ AUGUST 2007

SEPTEMBER 2007

OCTOBER 2007

NOVEMBER 2007

DECEMBER 2007

	THURSDAY	FRIDAY	SATURDAY
		1	2
	7	8	9
	14	15	16
	21	22	23
	28	29	30

⑥

⑦

2007

Monday,
June 4, 2007

④

Listen

Listen and point to
the words you hear.
Then point to each
item in the picture.
Listen again and
repeat each word.

1. calendar
2. year
3. month
4. date
5. day
6. week
7. weekend
8. clock
9. watch
10. morning
11. afternoon
12. evening

1 **Say It** Practice the conversation with a partner.

A: What time is it?

B: It's <u>one o'clock</u>.

A: <u>One o'clock</u>?

B: Yes, that's right.

A: Thank you.

Practice the conversation again. This time use the clocks below.

1. 4:00   2. 7:00   3. 11:00   4: 12:00

1:00   **1:05**   **1:15**

(one o'clock)   **(one oh five)**   **(one fifteen)**

1:30   **1:45**

(one thirty)   **(one forty-five)**

2 **Say It** Practice the conversation with a partner.

A: What time do you have?

B: <u>Two fifteen</u>.

A: I'm sorry. What time is it?

B: It's <u>two fifteen</u>.

A: Thank you.

Practice the conversation again. This time use the photos below.

1

2

3

3 **Listen and Write** Listen to the conversations. For each conversation, write the time you hear under the clock. Then draw the time on the clock.

1. _____ 2. _____ 3. _____ 4. _____

5. _____ 6. _____ 7. _____ 8. _____

4 **Pair Practice** Work with a partner. Point to a clock in Activity 3. Ask your partner what time it is. Ask about all of the clocks.

Example: *Student 1:* What time is it?
Student 2: It's 2:30.

5 **Listen** Listen to the ordinal numbers. Point to each number as you hear it and repeat the number.

January						
SUNDAY	MONDAY	TUESDAY	WEDNESDAY	THURSDAY	FRIDAY	SATURDAY
1 (1st)	2 (2nd)	3 (3rd)	4 (4th)	5 (5th)	6 (6th)	7 (7th)
8 (8th)	9 (9th)	10 (10th)	11 (11th)	12 (12th)	13 (13th)	14 (14th)
15 (15th)	16 (16th)	17 (17th)	18 (18th)	19 (19th)	20 (20th)	21 (21st)
22 (22nd)	23 (23rd)	24 (24th)	25 (25th)	26 (26th)	27 (27th)	28 (28th)
29 (29th)	30 (30th)	31 (31st)				

6 **Say It** Practice the conversation with a partner.

January						
SUNDAY	MONDAY	TUESDAY	WEDNESDAY	THURSDAY	FRIDAY	SATURDAY
1	2	3	4	5	6	7
8	9	10	11	12	13	14
15	16	17	18	19	20	21
22	23	24	25	26	27	28
29	30	31				

A: What day is it?
B: It's <u>Wednesday</u>.
A: What's the date?
B: Today is <u>January fourth</u>.

Practice the conversation again. This time, use the calendars below.

January						
SUNDAY	MONDAY	TUESDAY	WEDNESDAY	THURSDAY	FRIDAY	SATURDAY
1	2	3	4	5	6	7
8	9	10	11	12	13	14
15	16	17	18	19	20	21
22	23	24	25	26	27	28
29	30	31				

1

January						
SUNDAY	MONDAY	TUESDAY	WEDNESDAY	THURSDAY	FRIDAY	SATURDAY
1	2	3	4	5	6	7
8	9	10	11	12	13	14
15	16	17	18	19	20	21
22	23	24	25	26	27	28
29	30	31				

2

January						
SUNDAY	MONDAY	TUESDAY	WEDNESDAY	THURSDAY	FRIDAY	SATURDAY
1	2	3	4	5	6	7
8	9	10	11	12	13	14
15	16	17	18	19	20	21
22	23	24	25	26	27	28
29	30	31				

3

7 **Pair Practice** Work with a partner. Point to a box on a calendar on page 66. Ask your partner the day and date.

> **Note** Tell a *birthday* with month and day only.
> Tell a *date of birth* with month, day, and year.

8 **Say It** Practice the conversation with a partner.

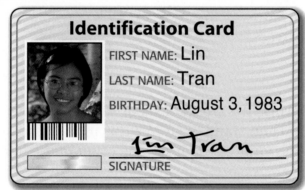

Identification Card
FIRST NAME: Lin
LAST NAME: Tran
BIRTHDAY: August 3, 1983
SIGNATURE

A: When is <u>Lin's</u> birthday?
B: Her birthday is <u>August third</u>.
A: What's her date of birth?
B: <u>August third, 1983</u>.

Practice the conversation again. This time use the ID cards below.

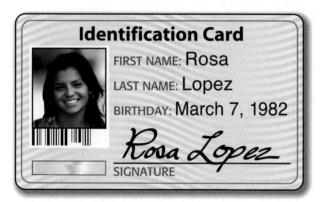

Identification Card
FIRST NAME: Rosa
LAST NAME: Lopez
BIRTHDAY: March 7, 1982
SIGNATURE

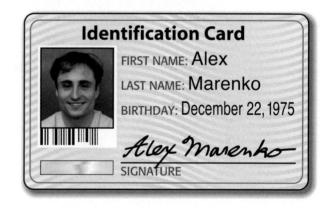

Identification Card
FIRST NAME: Alex
LAST NAME: Marenko
BIRTHDAY: December 22, 1975
SIGNATURE

Culture Tip

How Old Are You?

In the United States, it is not polite to ask adults their age. It is OK to ask children and teenagers their age.

Note In American English we write dates in this order: month, day, year.
There are two ways to write a date:
January 14, 2004 *or* 1/14/04

9 **Write** Write the dates below in numbers.

1. January 7, 2004   <u>1/07/04</u>   5. September 22, 1986   _____
2. March 19, 1998   _____   6. October 12, 2003   _____
3. November 11, 1954   _____   7. December 25, 1991   _____
4. June 3, 1995   _____   8. February 2, 2001   _____

10 **Group Practice** Work in a group of six or seven students. Tell each other your birthdays. Then stand or sit in a line in the time order of your birthdays. Tell the class your birthdays in the order of the line.

11 **Teamwork Task** Work in teams of four. Ask your teammates their birthdays. Write the name and birthday of each person in your group below. Then write the birthdays in time order. Begin with the birthday that is the closest to January 1.

NAME	BIRTHDAY	BIRTHDAYS IN TIME ORDER
_____	_____	1. _____
_____	_____	2. _____
_____	_____	3. _____
_____	_____	4. _____

Game Time

Guess your teacher's birthday. First guess the month. Then guess the day. Don't ask the year.

Every Day

1. Listen and Write Write the correct verbs under the pictures. Use the verbs in the box. Then listen to Cindy to check your answers.

| go | ~~get up~~ | take | eat | get | make | study | wash | brush |

Every day . . .

1. I _get up_ .

2. I _____ a shower.

3. I _____ my teeth.

4. I _____ dressed

5. I _____ my bed.

6. I _____ breakfast.

7. I _____ the dishes

8. I _____ .

9. I _____ to work.

2. Pair Practice Work with a partner. Ask and answer questions about Cindy's morning schedule.

Example: *Student 1:* What time does Cindy get up?
Student 2: She gets up at six o'clock.

> **Note** Use the simple present tense to talk about actions that happen regularly.
> **Examples:** I **take** a shower **every day**.
> He **cooks** dinner **every evening**.
> They **go** to the park **every Saturday**.

3 Write Answer the questions about your daily schedule.

What time do you . . .

1. get up? _I get up at 7:30_____ .
2. take a shower? _____ .
3. brush your teeth? _____ .
4. eat breakfast? _____ .
5. go to school or work? _____ .
6. eat lunch? _____ .

What else do you do every day? What time do you do it?

7. _____ .   9. _____ .

8. _____ .   10. _____ .

GRAMMAR CHECK

Simple present: Spelling changes with he, she, and it

Subject	Simple Present Verb	
I/you/we/they	wear brush study	Use the base verb with *I, you, we,* and *they.*
he/she/it	wear**s**	For most verbs, add -s when you use the verb with he, she, or it.
	brush**es**	For verbs that end in **s, ss, sh, ch, x,** or **z,** add -es.
	stud**ies**	For verbs that end in **y,** change the **y** to **i,** and add -es.

Check Point:

✓ Some verbs are irregular. Irregular verbs have different spelling changes:
have/has, do/does, go/goes

4 Write How are these verbs spelled with *he, she,* and *it*?

1. get _____   3. brush _____   5. go _____
2. take _____   4. eat _____   6. cry _____

5 Pair Practice Work with a partner. Ask your partner the questions in Activity 3. Write your partner's answers.

Example: *Student 1:* When do you get up?
 Student 2: I get up at 7:30.
 Jose gets up at 7:30.

1. _____   4. _____
2. _____   5. _____
3. _____   6. _____

6 **Say It** Practice the conversation with a partner.

go to the supermarket?
every Saturday

A: When does <u>she go to the supermarket</u>?

B: <u>She goes to the supermarket every Saturday</u>.

A: When do you <u>go to the supermarket</u>?

B: I <u>go to the supermarket</u> every . . .

Practice the conversation again. This time use the pictures below.

1. **study English?**
   every day

2. **call your family?**
   every week

3. **do your laundry?**
   every Sunday

7 **Pair Practice** Work with a partner. Ask your partner about his/her habits. Use the phrases below. Then write your partner's answers.

Example: *Student 1:* What do you do every morning?
Student 2: I take a shower every morning.
<u>Eva takes a shower every morning</u>.

1. Every morning? _____.

2. Every afternoon? _____.

3. Every evening? _____.

4. Every weekend? _____.

5. Every Sunday? _____.

6. Every summer? _____.

⑧ Problem Solving Work in groups of three or four. Look at the pictures of Alex's morning. What does Alex do first? What does he do second? Number the pictures from 1 to 6. Then write one of the times in the box under each picture.

| 8:00 | 8:10 | 8:15 | 8:30 | 8:45 | 9:00 |

Number _____

Time _____

Number _____

Time _____

Number _____1_____

Time _____8:00_____

Number _____

Time _____

Number _____

Time _____

Number _____

Time _____

⑨ Write On a piece of paper, write a story about Alex's morning. Begin with this sentence:

Every morning Alex gets up at 8:00.

Game Time

Tell your classmates a time of day. Your classmates will guess what you do at that time.

Example: Student 1: 12:00
Student 2: Do you eat lunch at 12:00?

Note AM means *in the morning.* PM means *in the afternoon, evening, or night.*

1 Say It Practice the conversation with a partner.

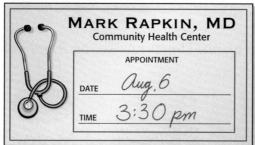

MARK RAPKIN, MD
Community Health Center

APPOINTMENT

DATE *Aug. 6*

TIME *3:30 pm*

A: When is your appointment with the doctor?

B: It's in <u>August</u>.

A: What's the date and time?

B: It's on <u>August sixth</u> at <u>3:30 in the afternoon</u>.

Practice the conversation again. This time use the appointment cards below.

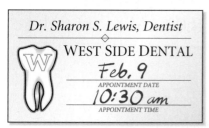

Dr. Sharon S. Lewis, Dentist

WEST SIDE DENTAL

Feb. 9
APPOINTMENT DATE

10:30 am
APPOINTMENT TIME

1

Ms. Ann Page
Counselor

The
Downtown
Adult
School

APPOINTMENT

Sept. 15
DATE

12:30 pm
TIME

2

Mr. John Cash
FINANCIAL AID OFFICER

IRVING COLLEGE

DATE *Nov. 3* TIME *9:45 am*
APPOINTMENT

3

Note Some months have abbreviations:

| Jan. = January | Aug. = August | Oct. = October | Dec. = December |
| Feb. = February | Sept. = September | Nov. = November | |

GRAMMAR CHECK

In/On/At/From . . . to for time

	Example	Explanation
in	**in** January / **in** 2001 / **in** the morning	Use **in** for a month, a year, or a part of the day.
on	**on** Monday / **on** April 29	Use **on** for a day or a date.
at	**at** 12:30 / **at** night	Use **at** for a specific time, and in the phrase *at night*.
from . . . to	**from** 9:00 **to** 5:00 / **from** Monday **to** Friday	Use **from . . . to** to talk about a period of time.

2 Say It Practice the conversation with a partner.

CITYWIDE BANK
OPEN
Monday–Friday
9:30 AM–5:00 PM

A: What days is the <u>bank</u> open?

B: From <u>Monday</u> to <u>Friday</u>.

A: What time?

B: From <u>9:30 in the morning</u> to <u>5:00 in the afternoon</u>.

Practice the conversation again. This time use the flyers below.

POST OFFICE
Monday–Friday   9:00 AM–5:00 PM
Saturday   9:00 AM–12:30 PM
Sunday Closed

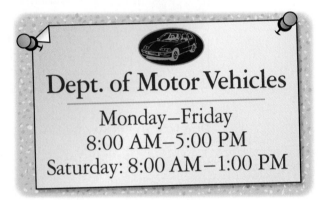

Dept. of Motor Vehicles
Monday–Friday
8:00 AM–5:00 PM
Saturday: 8:00 AM–1:00 PM

Community Health Center
Monday, Wednesday & Friday
10:00 AM–6:00 PM
Tuesday & Thursday
1:00 PM–7:00 PM
Saturday & Sunday
11:00 AM–3:00 PM

3 Listen Listen to Cindy describe her workday. Fill in the times you hear.

1. <u>8:15</u> : arrive at the supermarket

2. ____ : start work in the bakery

3. ____ : make coffee

4. ____ : put pastries on shelves

5. ____—____ : work in the bakery

6. ____—____ : have lunch

7. ____—____ : help out at the deli counter

8. ____ : clean up bakery and deli

9. ____ : sweep the floor

10. ____ : leave work and go to school

Shop & Save Supermarket Employee Schedule

	8:00–9:00	9:00–10:00	10:00–11:00	11:00–12:00	12:00–1:00	1:00–2:00	2:00–3:00	3:00–4:00	4:00–5:00
Mon.	A	A	A	A	A		A	A	
Tues.	A	A	A	A	A R	R	A R	A R	R
Wed.	A	A	A	A	A R	R	A R	A R	R
Thurs.	A C	A C	A	A C	A R	R C	A R C	A R	R
Fri.	A C	A C	A C	A C	A R	R C	A R C	A R	R
Sat.	C	C	C	C	R	R C	R C	R	R
Sun.	C	C	C	C	R	R C	R C	R	R

A=Alberto   R=Rosa   C=Cindy

4 **Pair Practice** With a partner, ask and answer the questions about the work schedules.

1. What days does Alberto work? _____
2. What hours does Alberto work? _____
3. What time does Alberto have lunch? _____
4. Does Alberto work full time or part time? _____
5. What days does Rosa work? _____
6. What time does Rosa start work? _____
7. What day does Rosa have "off"? _____
8. What days does Cindy work? _____
9. Does Cindy work full time? _____
10. What time does Cindy start work? _____

Culture Tip

Full-time / Part-time

In the United States, a job that is seven hours a day or thirty-five hours a week is a full-time job. A job that is less time is a part-time job.

5 **Pair Practice** Work with a partner. Ask and answer questions about the Shop & Save employee schedule. Ask as many questions as you can.

6 **Say It** Practice the conversation with a partner.

NAME:	Hector Domingo
JOB:	Bus Driver
DAYS:	Mon.-Fri.
HOURS:	7:00 am - 4:00 pm
DUTIES:	Drive a bus

A: What is <u>Hector's</u> job?

B: He's a <u>bus driver</u>.

A: When does <u>he</u> work?

B: He works from <u>Monday to Friday</u>.

A: What time does <u>he</u> work?

B: He works from 7:00 AM to 4:00 PM.

A: What does <u>he</u> do every day?

B: <u>He drives a bus</u>.

Practice the conversation again. This time use the information below.

NAME:	Sarah Chung
JOB:	Waitress
DAYS:	Tues.-Sun.
HOURS:	10:00am-7:00pm
DUTIES:	take orders and serve food

NAME:	Carmen Diaz
JOB:	Receptionist
DAYS:	Mon., Wed., and Fri.
HOURS:	10:00am-6:00pm
DUTIES:	greet people and answer the phone

NAME:	Alex Marenko
JOB:	Salesperson
DAYS:	Wed.-Sun.
HOURS:	2:00pm - 9:00pm
DUTIES:	sell computers

7 **Teamwork Task** Work in teams of four. Ask your teammates about jobs they have now, or jobs they want, if they don't have jobs now. Write the information below.

	STUDENT 1	STUDENT 2	STUDENT 3
Name:			
Job:			
Days:			
Hours:			
Duties:			

Homework

Ask someone in your family or a neighbor about their job. Ask about the days and hours they work and their duties. Report back to the class.

Review

1 **Listen and Read** Listen to the story. Then read the story.

Many Kinds of Jobs

My husband, Hector, gets up at six o'clock every morning. He takes a quick shower, brushes his teeth, and gets dressed. He drinks a cup of coffee and goes to work at 6:30. At work, he drives a bus all day.

My sister Rosa gets up at eight o'clock. She takes a long shower. She drinks a cup of tea. Then she rides her bicycle to the park. She doesn't go to work in the morning. She eats lunch at home. Then she goes to work in the afternoon. She is a cashier. She works at the Shop & Save supermarket.

I don't have a job, but I work at home every day. I am a homemaker. Every morning I get up early. I cook breakfast for my children before they go to school. At eight o'clock I take my children to school. In the afternoon I clean our apartment, buy groceries, and study English. I don't work in an office, but I have a full-time job at home!

2 **Write** Read the questions. Write the answers.

1. What time does Hector get up? _____.
2. What does Hector do all day? _____.
3. Who gets up at 8:00? _____.
4. What does Rosa drink every morning? _____.
5. Where does Rosa eat lunch? _____.
6. What time do Angela's children go to school? _____.
7. What does Angela do in the afternoon? _____.
8. Where does Angela work? _____.

INTERNET IDEA

Search the Internet for information about a U.S. holiday, like *July 4th, Thanksgiving, or President's Day*. When is the holiday? How do people in the U.S. celebrate the holiday? Tell your classmates about the holiday.

Alberto's Saturdays

My Saturdays are very busy. Every Saturday I work in my brother's restaurant. I get up at 5:00 in the morning. I stay in bed for a few minutes. Then I take a shower at about 5:15. Then at 5:30 I get dressed. I leave my house at 6:00. I don't eat breakfast at home. I eat breakfast at the restaurant at 6:45. Then I start work at 7:00. I eat lunch at 1:30 and finish work at 4:00.

④ **Group Practice** Work in groups of three or four. Fill out the Saturday schedule for Alberto.

TIME	ACTIVITY	TIME	ACTIVITY
5:00	Alberto gets up .	_____	_____ .
_____	_____ .	_____	_____ .
_____	_____ .	_____	_____ .
_____	_____ .	_____	_____ .

⑤ **Write** Choose a day during the week. Fill out your schedule for that day.

TIME	ACTIVITY	TIME	ACTIVITY
_____	_____ .	_____	_____ .
_____	_____ .	_____	_____ .
_____	_____ .	_____	_____ .
_____	_____ .	_____	_____ .

⑥ **Pair Practice** With a partner, ask and answer questions to complete George's Monday Schedule. Student 1 looks at the schedule on this page. Student 2 looks at the schedule on the next page.

Example: *Student 1:* What does George do at 7:40?
Student 2: He takes a shower.

GEORGE'S MONDAY SCHEDULE

7:30	gets up
7:40	takes a shower
8:00	brushes his teeth
8:10	
8:20	cooks and eats breakfast
8:45	

GEORGE'S MONDAY SCHEDULE

TIME	ACTIVITY
7:30	
7:40	takes a shower
8:00	
8:10	drinks tea
8:20	
8:45	washes the dishes

7 **Best Answer** Bubble the correct answer.

                                                                   a   **b**

1. What time is it?

   a) It's Monday.   **b)** It's 4:30.   ○   ●

2. When is your appointment?

   a) At Friday.   **b)** On Friday.   ○   ○

3. His date of birth is 7/11/85. He was born in _____

   a) July.   **b)** September.   ○   ○

4. What does she do at 9:00 in the morning?

   a) She eats breakfast.   **b)** She eat breakfast.   ○   ○

5. What does he do every day?

   a) He studys English.   **b)** He studies English.   ○   ○

8 **Write** Write the words for the numbered items in the picture.

① DECEMBER ③					⑤ 2006 ②	
SUNDAY	MONDAY	TUESDAY	WEDNESDAY	THURSDAY	FRIDAY ⑤	SATURDAY
					1	2
3	4	5	6	7	8	9 ⑥
10	11	12	13	14	15 ④	16
17	18	19	20	21	22	23
24	25	26	27	28	29	30
31						

1. calendar   4. _____

2. _____   5. _____

3. _____   6. _____

Pronunciation Time

A. Listen to and repeat each of these times.

| 12:15 | 12:50 | 8:13 | 8:30 | 7:14 | 7:40 |

B. Listen and write the times you hear.

1. _____ 2. _____ 3. _____ 4. _____

⑨ Teamwork Task

A. With your team, learn more about the jobs of the workers in your school. Work in pairs to interview one worker at your school. One student should ask the questions, and the other should write down the worker's answers. Don't forget to ask these questions.

- What is your job?
- What days of the week do you work?
- What hours do you work?
- What are your job duties?

B. Report back to your team and work together to prepare a presentation about the school jobs your team learned about.

C. Give your presentation to the class.

I can . . .			
• ask for and tell the time.	1	2	3
• say and write times and dates.	1	2	3
• put dates in time order.	1	2	3
• say and write my date of birth.	1	2	3
• use ordinal numbers.	1	2	3
• talk about daily activities.	1	2	3
• read and understand an appointment card.	1	2	3
• read and understand a work schedule.	1	2	3
• use prepositions of time.	1	2	3
• understand simple present spelling changes with *he, she,* and *it.*	1	2	3

1 = not well   2 = OK   3 = very well

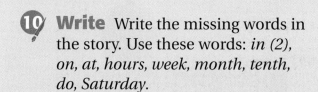

10 **Write** Write the missing words in the story. Use these words: *in (2), on, at, hours, week, month, tenth, do, Saturday.*

Alberto: When is your birthday, Cindy?
Cindy: My birthday is (1)_____ April.

Alberto: That's nice. April is my favorite
(2)_____.
Cindy: It's (3)_____ April (4)_____.

Cindy: Is your job full time? How many
(5)_____ do you work?
Alberto: I work forty hours a
(6)_____. How about you?

Cindy: I get up very early. I start work
(7)_____ 5:30 (8)_____ the
morning.
Alberto: Wow. That is early

Alberto: But tomorrow is
(9)_____. You don't go to work on
Saturdays, do you?

Alberto: What's the matter, Cindy?
Cindy: It's late, Alberto. And I (10)_____
work on Saturdays. So, it's time to go.
Alberto: OK. Let's go.

11 **Pair Practice** Practice the story with a partner.

Busy Lives

GOALS

- ✓ Talk about activities at home
- ✓ Talk about recreational activities
- ✓ Talk about work activities
- ✓ Pay a bill
- ✓ Balance a checkbook
- ✓ Identify common jobs
- ✓ Identify the tools of different jobs
- ✓ Use the present continuous

Listen

Listen and point to the action words you hear. Then point to the person or animal in the picture doing each action. Listen again and repeat each word.

  1. cooking
  2. eating
  3. giving
  4. taking
  5. drinking
  6. singing
  7. dancing
  8. listening
  9. sleeping
 10. throwing
 11. jumping
 12. selling
 13. buying
 14. swimming
 15. walking
 16. flying
 17. working

At Home

1 **Say It** Practice the conversation with a partner.

get dressed

A: What time is it?
B: It's <u>seven o'clock</u>.
A: Where is Angela?
B: She's at home.
A: What is she doing?
B: She's <u>getting dressed.</u>

Practice the conversation again. This time use the pictures below.

1. **make the bed**

2. **talk on the phone**

3. **do laundry**

2 **Write** Match the letters to the numbers to make complete sentences.

1. She is cooking . . .   ___E___   A. a book.

2. I am watching . . .   _____   B. to music.

3. He is taking . . ..   _____   C. the dishes.

4. She is reading . .   _____   D. television.

5. They are talking . . .   _____   ~~E.~~ dinner.

6. She is brushing . . .   _____   F. her teeth.

7. He is washing . . .   _____   G. on the telephone.

8. We are listening . . .   _____   H. a shower.

Present continuous: Statements

Subject	be	Verb + ing
I	am	eating.
You / We / They	are	sleeping.
He / She / It	is	studying.

Check Points:
- ✓ The present continuous tells about things happening right now.
- ✓ Negative present continuous:
  I am **not** eating. I am **not** sleeping.

3 **Write** Look at the pictures. Write a sentence about what each person is doing.

1. <u>She is brushing her teeth</u> .

2. _____ .

3. _____ .

4. _____ .

5. _____ .

6. <u>I am . . .</u> .

4 **Say it** Practice the conversation with a partner.

A: Where <u>is</u> <u>Hector</u>?
B: <u>He's</u> at home.
A: What <u>is he</u> doing?
B: <u>He's washing dishes and listening to music</u>.

Hector / wash dishes / listen to music

Practice the conversation again. This time use the pictures below.

1. **Juan / watch TV / eat grapes**

2. **Angela and Rosa / drink coffee / talk**

3. **Gloria and the dog / sleep / dream**

5 **Pair Practice** Ask and answer questions about what the people in Activity 4 are wearing.

Example: *Student 1:* What's Hector wearing?
Student 2: He's wearing blue jeans and a gray shirt.

6 **Group Practice** Work with a group of five or six students. Choose an activity that you do at home like cooking, eating, or washing dishes. Pretend to do this activity. The other students in the group will guess what activity you are doing. Take turns.

7 **Pair Practice** Work with a partner. Look at the people in the picture on pages 82–83. Say what each person is doing.

8 **Write** Write a present continuous sentence about each picture. Use the verbs in the box. Some verbs may be used more than once.

look	put	deduct	write	mail

Note Deduct means subtract.

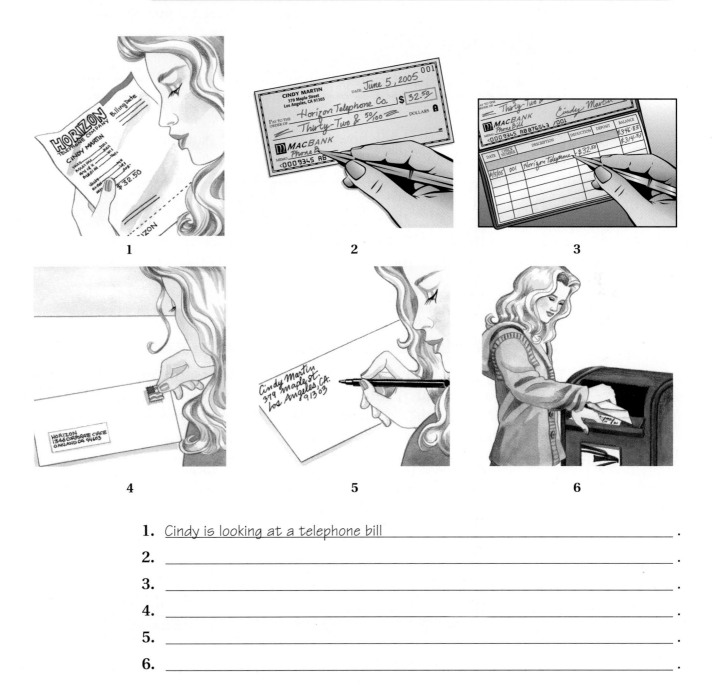

1   2   3

4   5   6

1. <u>Cindy is looking at a telephone bill</u>   .

2. _____ .

3. _____ .

4. _____ .

5. _____ .

6. _____ .

9 **Pair Practice** Explain to your partner how to pay a bill. (Try not to look at Activity 8!)

10 Write Write a check to the Horizon Telephone Company for a $44.82 bill.

379 Maple Street
Los Angeles, CA 91303

DATE: _____

001

PAY TO THE
ORDER OF _____ $ [   ]

_____ DOLLARS 🔒

ⓂMACBANK

MEMO _____   MP

⑆000 9345 ⑈ AB 876543 ⑆001

11 Problem Solving Look how Cindy deducted (subtracted) her check from her checkbook.

DATE	CHECK NUMBER	DESCRIPTION	DEDUCTION	DEPOSIT	BALANCE
					$346.⁸³
6/5/05	001	Horizon Telephone	-$32.⁵⁰		$314.³³

This is your checkbook. Look at the *balance* (the amount of money you have in your account). Then *deduct* (subtract) your check from the balance, and write the new balance. Don't forget to write the date, the check number, and the description.

DATE	CHECK NUMBER	DESCRIPTION	DEDUCTION	DEPOSIT	BALANCE
					$289.⁷⁵

Homework

Choose a time at home. Write a sentence about what each person in your home is doing at that moment.

On Vacation

1 **Say It** Practice the conversation with a partner.

in the pool / swim

A: Where are Rosa and Cindy?
B: They are <u>in the pool</u>.
A: What are they doing?
B: They're <u>swimming</u>.

Practice the conversation again. This time use the pictures below.

1. **in a nightclub / dance**

2. **in the mountains / hike**

3. **in a museum /
look at paintings**

2 **Listen** The Domingo family is on vacation. Listen to the different things they are doing on their vacation. Choose one of the words in the box for each activity you hear.

sleeping	dancing	eating	running	shopping	swimming

1. _____ 4. _____

2. _____ 5. _____

3. _____ 6. _____

3 **Write** Answer the questions about the Domingo family's schedule.

The Domingo Family's Vacation Schedule

Monday: hike in the mountains **Friday:** play tennis
Tuesday: drive in the country **Saturday:** shop
Wednesday: visit museums **Sunday:** relax at the beach
Thursday: walk around town

1. It's Monday. What are they doing? _____.

2. Now it's Tuesday. What are they doing? _____.

3. Now it's Wednesday. What are they doing? _____.

4. Now it's Thursday. What are they doing? _____.

5. Now it's Friday. What are they doing? _____.

6. Now it's Saturday. What are they doing? _____.

7. Now it's Sunday. What are they doing? _____.

4 **Say It** Practice the conversation with a partner.

play baseball?/ play tennis

A: <u>Are they playing baseball</u>?
B: No, <u>they aren't</u>.
A: What <u>are they</u> doing?
B: <u>They're playing tennis</u>.

Practice the conversation again. This time use the pictures below.

1. sleep? / eat   2. swim? / relax   3. we / watch TV? / practice English

Culture Tip

Sports
Basketball is the most popular sport in the U.S.

Present continuous yes/no questions and short answers

Be	Subject	Verb + ing	Short Answers	
			Yes	No
Am	I	eating?	**Yes,** you **are.**	**No,** you **aren't.**
Are	you	drinking?	**Yes,** I **am.**	**No,** I**'m not.**
Is	he/she/it	dancing?	**Yes,** he **is.**	**No,** he/she/it **isn't.**
Are	we/they	relaxing?	**Yes,** we/they **are.**	**No,** we/they **aren't.**

5 **Group Practice** Work in groups of three or four. Pretend you are on vacation. Write a present continuous sentence about what you are doing.
(**Example:** I am swimming in a pool.)

Don't tell the other students your sentence. Ask questions to find out what the other students in your group are doing.
(**Example:** Are you eating?)

When you guess each student's activity, write the person's name and activity in the chart.

NAME	WHAT HE OR SHE IS DOING
_____	_____
_____	_____
_____	_____
_____	_____

6 **Write** Change the statements to *yes/no* questions.

1. They are swimming in the pool.   Are they swimming in the pool ?
2. I am having lunch.   _____ ?
3. My children are dancing.   _____ ?
4. I am exercising.   _____ ?
5. We are listening to music.   _____ ?
6. She is buying T-shirts.   _____ ?

7 **Say It** Practice the conversation with a partner.

A: Hi, Mom. It's me, Cindy.

B: Hi, Cindy. Where are you calling from?

A: I'm calling from <u>New York City</u>.

B: What are you doing in <u>New York City</u>?

A: I'm <u>taking pictures of the Statue of Liberty</u>.

B: That sounds exciting!

**New York City /
take pictures of the Statue of Liberty**

Practice the conversation again. This time use the pictures below.

**1. Hollywood /
meet movie stars**

**2. Arizona /
look at the Grand Canyon**

**3. Washington D.C. /
visit the White House**

8 **Teamwork Task** Work in teams of three or four. Talk about good places to go on vacation. Write the names of three places below. Write things you can do in each place.

PLACE	ACTIVITY
1. <u>Washington, D.C.</u>	<u>go to museums, visit monuments, see the White House</u>
2. _____	_____
3. _____	_____
4. _____	_____

Homework

Find one or two pictures in a newspaper or magazine of a person doing something fun. Bring your pictures to class and tell your class what the people in the pictures are doing.

At Work

1 **Say It** Practice the conversation with a partner.

greet a patient

A: Is Carmen working?
B: Yes, she is.
A: What is she doing?
B: She's <u>greeting a patient</u>.

Practice the conversation again. This time use the pictures below.

1. **answer the phone**

2. **take a message**

3. **take a break**

2 **Write** Finish each sentence with one of the choices in the box. Use the present continuous.

| drive a bus | ~~serve food~~ | give a customer change |
| cash a check | answer the phone | help a customer |

1. Sarah is a waitress. Right now . . .   <u>she is serving food</u>.
2. Hector is a bus driver. Right now . . .   _____ .
3. Rosa is a cashier. Right now . . .   _____ .
4. Carmen is a receptionist. Right now . . .   _____ .
5. Alex is a salesperson. Right now . . .   _____ .
6. Lin is a bank teller. Right now . . . .   _____ .

3 **Say It** Practice the conversation with a partner.

A: Is the <u>mechanic</u> using a
   <u>hammer</u>?

B: No, <u>he</u> isn't using <u>a hammer</u>.

A: What is <u>he</u> using?

B: <u>He's</u> using a <u>screwdriver</u>.

**mechanic / hammer? /
screwdriver**

Practice the conversation again. This time use the pictures below.

1. **painter/ toothbrush? /
   paintbrush**

2. **manager /
   cash register? / computer**

3. **housekeeper / broom? /
   mop**

4 **Problem Solving** Match the job to the tool.

___ 1. receptionist   **a.** pots and pans

___ 2. mechanic   **b.** chalk

___ 3. hairstylist   **c.** telephone

___ 4. teacher   **d.** wrench

___ 5. cook   **e.** thermometer

___ 6. doctor   **f.** scissors

5 **Write** Irma is a housekeeper. Complete the story about Irma's workday. Use these words: *from, busy, housekeeper, are, works, days, to, helps, children.*

Irma Moran is a (1)_____ . She (2)_____ five (3)_____ a week, (4)_____ Monday (5)_____ Friday, for the Casey family. Mr. and Mrs. Casey (6)_____ both doctors. They are very (7)_____. Irma (8)_____ Mr. and Mrs. Casey take care of their home and their two (9)_____.

6 **Listen and Write** Listen to Irma talk about her job. Write the things that are missing from her work schedule.

7:00	Arrive at the Casey house	9:30	_____
7:15	Help the children get dressed	11:30	Take a break
7:30	_____	12:30	Buy groceries
7:40	Feed the children	1:30	_____
7:50	Take the children to school	2:30	Pick up the kids from school
9:00	_____	3:00	_____

Culture Tip

Break time

Most jobs in the U.S. give workers a break after four hours of work. Some jobs pay workers for their break time, but some jobs don't. In your country do workers get breaks? Do they get paid for break time?

7 **Pair Practice** Ask and answer questions about Irma's workday.

Example: *Student 1:* It's 12:45. What is Irma doing?
Student 2: She's buying groceries

8 **Group Work** Work with a group of five or six students. Choose a job. Pretend to do this job. The other students in your group will guess what job you are doing. Take turns.

⑨ Group Practice

A. Work in groups of three. Talk about the picture. Where is this? Who is in the picture? What are the people doing? Take five minutes to study the picture. Try to remember everything you can. Then close your books.

B. Take out a piece of paper. Work with your group to write sentences about the picture. Try to remember what the people are doing. Write as many sentences as you can.

Homework

Find one or two pictures in a newspaper or magazine of people doing their jobs. Bring your pictures to class and tell your class what the person in each picture is doing and what the person's job is.

Review

1 Listen and Read Listen to the story.
Then read the story.

A Busy Day

It is three o'clock on Monday afternoon and many things are happening in my neighborhood. Parents are picking up their children from school. People are buying groceries at the supermarket. At the clinic, the doctor and the nurse are helping patients and Carmen is answering the phone.

I'm not working in the clinic or in a restaurant. I am at home, but I'm busy, too. Right now I'm washing the dishes, doing the laundry, and taking care of my kids, all at the same time.

My neighbors, George and Sarah Chung, aren't working in their restaurant today. They're on vacation. They are at the beach right now. Maybe they're swimming. Or maybe they're sitting in the sun and relaxing. I don't know what they're doing, but I'm sure they are busy having a good time!

2 Write Answer the questions about the story.

1. What time is it? _____.

2. What are parents doing at the school? _____.

3. What are people doing at the supermarket? _____.

4. What is happening at the clinic? _____.

5. Where is Angela? _____.

6. What is Angela doing? _____.

7. Where are Mr. and Mrs. Chung? _____.

8. What are Mr. and Mrs. Chung probably doing? _____.

INTERNET IDEA

Use the Internet to find out about a vacation place. Use *vacation* or *tourism* as your search word. Also type in the name of the vacation place (for example, *Florida* or *Rome*.) Where is the vacation place? What is the weather like? What can you do there? Tell your class about the vacation place.

3 **Best Response** Bubble the correct answers.

a   b

1. What are you doing?

    a) I study English.   **b)** I'm studying English.   ○   ●

2. The receptionist is . . .

    a) answering the phone.   **b)** answers the phone.   ○   ○

3. Are you paying the bill?

    a) Yes, I'm writing a check now.   **b)** Yes, I'm calling now.   ○   ○

4. What are they doing on vacation?

    a) They're paying bills.   **b)** They're relaxing.   ○   ○

5. The painter is using . . .

    a) a paintbrush.   **b)** a computer.   ○   ○

4 **Write** Write the words for what each person in the picture is doing.

1. *cooking* _____   6. _____

2. _____   7. _____

3. _____   8. _____

4. _____   9. _____

5. _____

5 **Write** What are you doing right now? What do you think your family members, friends, and neighbors are doing? Write as many sentences as you can.

_____

_____

_____

_____

_____

_____

_____

6 **Problem Solving** Fill in the missing information in the checkbook. Remember to add *additions* and subtract *deductions*.

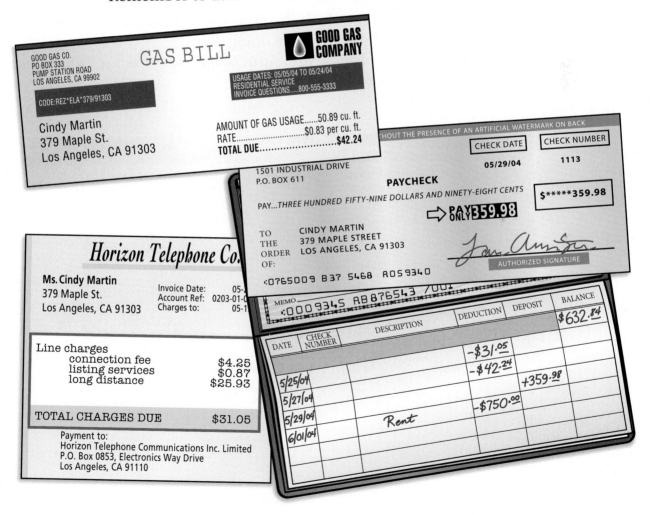

GAS BILL

GOOD GAS CO.
PO BOX 333
PUMP STATION ROAD
LOS ANGELES, CA 99902

CODE:REZ*ELA*379/91303

Cindy Martin
379 Maple St.
Los Angeles, CA 91303

GOOD GAS COMPANY

USAGE DATES: 05/05/04 TO 05/24/04
RESIDENTIAL SERVICE
INVOICE QUESTIONS.....800-555-3333

AMOUNT OF GAS USAGE......50.89 cu. ft.
RATE..............................$0.83 per cu. ft.
TOTAL DUE........................$42.24

Horizon Telephone Co.

Ms. Cindy Martin
379 Maple St.
Los Angeles, CA 91303

Invoice Date: 05-
Account Ref: 0203-01-0
Charges to: 05-1

Line charges
    connection fee $4.25
    listing services $0.87
    long distance $25.93

TOTAL CHARGES DUE $31.05

Payment to:
Horizon Telephone Communications Inc. Limited
P.O. Box 0853, Electronics Way Drive
Los Angeles, CA 91110

1501 INDUSTRIAL DRIVE
P.O. BOX 611

CHECK DATE | CHECK NUMBER
05/29/04 | 1113

PAYCHECK

PAY...THREE HUNDRED FIFTY-NINE DOLLARS AND NINETY-EIGHT CENTS

$*****359.98

PAY ONLY 359.98

TO THE ORDER OF:
CINDY MARTIN
379 MAPLE STREET
LOS ANGELES, CA 91303

AUTHORIZED SIGNATURE

‹0765009 837 5468 A059340

MEMO ‹0009345 AB876543 7001

DATE	CHECK NUMBER	DESCRIPTION	DEDUCTION	DEPOSIT	BALANCE
					$632.84
			-$31.05		
5/25/04			-$42.24		
5/27/04				+359.98	
5/29/04			-$750.00		
6/01/04		Rent			

Pronunciation /j/ and /y/

A. Listen and repeat the words with the /j/ sound.

job   jump   jar   jeans   just

B. Listen and repeat the words with the /y/ sound.

you   yellow   young   yes   your

C. Listen to the pairs of words. Practice them with a partner.

jet — yet   jam — yam   jell — yell   jeer — year

7 Teamwork Task

A. Work in teams of four or five. Choose either home, work, or vacation. With your group discuss things that people do in the place you chose.

B. Make up a skit about a day in the place you chose. Give each student a part to play. Your skit should have actions but no words. Practice the skit together.

C. Perform the skit for the class. The class will say what actions the people in your group are doing as you're doing them.

Example: *Marco is waking up. Maria is making breakfast. Now Marco is walking into the kitchen . . . .*

I can . . .			
• talk about activities I do at home.	1	2	3
• talk about recreational activities.	1	2	3
• talk about work activities.	1	2	3
• pay a bill.	1	2	3
• balance a checkbook.	1	2	3
• identify common jobs.	1	2	3
• identify the tools of different jobs.	1	2	3
• use the present continuous.	1	2	3

1 = not well   2 = OK   3 = very well

Rosa: Hi, Cindy. what are you (1)_____?
Cindy: I'm just (2)_____ here and
(3)_____ coffee.

Rosa: Really? What else are you doing?
Cindy: Well, I'm also (4)_____.

Rosa: What are you thinking about? Or
should I say, (5)_____ (6)_____ you
thinking about?

Cindy: Alberto. He is on vacation in the
mountains. (7)_____ skiing with his
brother.
Rosa: Oh. I understand.

Rosa: How long (8)_____ (9)_____
staying in the mountains?
Cindy: Four days.
Rosa: Why don't you call him?
Cindy: I don't know, Rosa.
Rosa: Cindy, call him!

Cindy: Alberto? It's me. Cindy.
Alberto: Cindy! I was just (10)_____
about you.
Cindy: Really?
Alberto: Really!
Cindy: That's nice.

9 **Group Practice** Work in groups of three. Practice the story.

The Community

GOALS

- ✓ Identify neighborhood places
- ✓ Describe locations
- ✓ Ask for and give directions
- ✓ Read and understand maps
- ✓ Talk about your neighborhood
- ✓ Identify and talk about neighborhood jobs
- ✓ Use *in, on,* and *at* for place
- ✓ Use adjectives to describe people
- ✓ Contrast simple present and present continuous tense

Listen 🎧

Listen and point to the words you hear. Then point to each item in the picture. Listen again and repeat each word.

1. library
2. post office
3. gas station
4. hair salon
5. drugstore
6. clinic
7. parking lot
8. bus station
9. bookstore
10. café
11. apartment building
12. park
13. mail carrier
14. mechanic
15. doctor
16. hairstylist
17. police officer
18. street sign

1 Say It Practice the conversation with a partner.

A: Excuse me.

B: Yes?

A: Where is the <u>post office</u>?

B: It's on <u>Elm Street, around the corner from the supermarket</u>.

A: <u>On Elm Street, around the corner from the supermarket</u>. Thank you very much.

B: You're welcome.

post office?

Practice the conversation again. This time use the pictures below.

1. **drugstore?**   2. **bookstore?**   3. **café?**

2 Group Practice Work in groups of three or four. Make a list of places in your school's neighborhood. Write the street each place is on. Then describe the location of the place. You can use a local map to help you.

PLACE	STREET	DESCRIPTION OF LOCATION
drugstore	Charles St.	next to the police station

3 **Pair Practice** Work with a partner. Look at the picture of Angela's neighborhood on pages 102–103. Ask about locations of places in Angela's neighborhood.

Example: *Student 1:* Where is the hair salon?
Student 2: It's on Third Street, between the gas station and the drugstore.

Word Help: Directions/locations

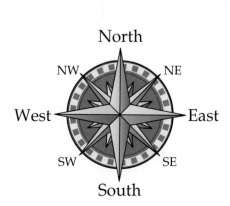

North
NW NE
West — East
SW SE
South

turn right / go straight / turn left

on the corner of
(Davis St. and Gavin St.)

4 **Pair Practice** Look at the picture of Angela's neighborhood on pages 102–103. Work with a partner to circle the right answers.

1. Second Street runs north and south / east and west.

2. Avenue C runs north and south / east and west.

3. You are at the café. The park is north / east.

4. You are at the library. The park is north / west.

5. You are at the drugstore. To go to the park you turn left / turn right.

6. You are at the bookstore. To go to the café you turn left / turn right.

7. You are at the gas station. To go to the drugstore you turn left / go straight.

8. The post office is on the corner of Second St. and Third St. / Third St. and Ave. B.

Culture Tip

City life
More than 80% of the people in the United States live in or near cities.

5 **Write** Make a list of things you can get or use at each of these neighborhood places.

1. drugstore: *medicine, shampoo,* _____

2. library: _____

3. post office: _____

4. supermarket: _____

6 **Listen** Look at the map. Listen to the directions. Put the places below in the correct boxes on the map. Write only the first letter of each place (Example: bus station = **b**).

bus station   **s**chool   **l**ibrary   **p**ark   **c**omputer store

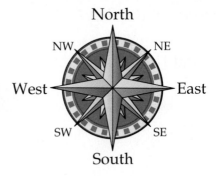

7 **Pair Practice** Explain to your partner how to get to each of the places in Activity 6.

Commuting

Your commute is the distance you travel from home to work or from home to school. The average American commutes twenty-six minutes each way. How long is your commute?

8 **Write** Fill in the blanks with the words and phrases in the box.

Excuse me	on	Thank you	north
turn	corner	Avenue J	bus station

A: _____. I'm looking for the _____.

B: It's _____ 22nd Street.

A: How can I get there from here?

B: Go _____ on _____ to 22nd Street. Then _____ right. It's on the _____ of Avenue J and 22nd Street.

A: _____ very much.

9 **Pair Practice** Practice the conversation in Activity 8 with a partner. Then ask for and give directions to places in the picture of Angela's neighborhood on pages 102–103.

GRAMMAR CHECK

in/on/at for place

	Example	Explanation
in	**in** Chicago **in** Mexico **in** apartment 12	Use **in** for a city, state, country, neighborhood, or apartment number.
on	**on** Tucker Street **on** the third floor	Use **on** for a street or a floor.
at	**at** 112 Clark Street **at** Bob's Café	Use **at** for an address or name of a specific place.

10 **Say It** Practice the conversation with a partner.

A: Where do you live?

B: I live in <u>Brooklyn Heights</u>.

A: What street do you live on?

B: I live on <u>Hicks Street</u>.

A: What's your address?

B: I live at <u>112 Hicks Street</u>.

Practice the conversation again. This time use the pictures below.

1

2

3

11 **Teamwork Task** Work in teams of four. Ask your teammates where they live. Fill out the chart below for yourself and your team.

NAME	LIVES IN (NEIGHBORHOOD):	LIVES ON (STREET):	LIVES AT (ADDRESS):

Game Time

Put a blindfold on a volunteer. Hide an object (like an eraser or a dictionary). Give the volunteer directions (Ex: *turn right, turn left, go straight*) to help him or her find the object.

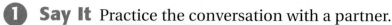
1 **Say It** Practice the conversation with a partner.

A: Do you know Angela's neighbor, <u>Tania</u>?

B: I'm not sure. Where does <u>she</u> live?

A: <u>She</u> lives <u>in Apartment 202</u>.

B: What does <u>she</u> look like?

A: <u>She's short</u> and <u>she</u> has <u>blond</u> hair.

Tania / short / blond

Practice the conversation again. This time use the pictures below.

1. **Cindy / tall / blond**

2. **Henri / very tall / black**

3. **Sarah / short / brown**

Word Help: Adjectives for people

tall / short

heavy / thin

long / short hair

blond / red / brown / black / gray hair

curly / wavy / straight hair

> **Note:** In English, put adjectives before nouns.
> I have brown eyes. *Not:* I have eyes brown.

2 **Pair Practice** Work with a partner. Student 1 describes someone in your class. Student 2 tries to guess who Student 1 is describing.

3 **Teamwork Task** Work in teams of four. Fill in the chart with information about each person on your team.

NAME:	HEIGHT: Tall/Short	HAIR: Long/Short	HAIR: Curly/Straight	EYES: Color

> **Note:** not tall or short = average height
> hair that is not long or short hair = medium length hair

Culture Tip

The average American
The average American man is 5 feet 8 inches tall. The average American woman is 5 feet 4 inches tall. The average American man weighs 176 pounds. The average American woman weighs 143 pounds.

GRAMMAR CHECK

Sentences with adjectives: *Be* vs. *have*

Subject + *be* + adjective	Subject + *have/has* + adjective + noun
He **is** tall.	He **has** short hair.
I **am** happy.	I **have** good neighbors.

Check Point:
✓ Use *be* in sentences with an adjective. Use *have/has* in sentences with a noun + adjective.

Write Write sentences with adjectives about the people in the photos. For each photo write one sentence with *be* and one sentence with *have*.

1. (height / hair color)

She is tall   .

She has gray hair   .

2. (weight / hair color)

_____ .

_____ .

3. (weight / eye color)

_____ .

_____ .

4. (weight / hair color)

_____ .

_____ .

5. (weight / hair length)

_____ .

_____ .

6. (weight / hair length)

_____ .

_____ .

5 **Listen** Listen and write one of these names under each person in the picture: *Debbie, Jahmal, Barbara, Hoshi, Rags, Steve.*

_____   _____   _____

_____   _____

6 **Pair Practice** Ask and answer questions about people in the picture.

Example: *Student 1*: Is Barbara tall?
                Student 2: Yes, she is.
                Student 1: Does Barbara have brown hair?
                Student 2: No, she doesn't.

7 **Teamwork Task** Work in teams of three. On a piece of paper, write sentences about the people in the picture. Write as many sentences as you can. Then read your sentences to the class.

> ### Game Time
>
> Your teacher will write the name of a student on a piece of paper. Ask questions with adjectives to try to guess who the student is.
>
> **Example:**   Is it a woman? Is she tall? Does she have long hair?

Homework

Write descriptions of your friends and family.

Example: My brother is tall. He has short hair.

Neighborhood Jobs

1 **Say It** Practice the conversation with a partner.

A: What does <u>he</u> do?

B: <u>He's</u> a <u>baker</u>. He <u>bakes bread</u>.

A: What is <u>he</u> doing now?

B: <u>He's</u> <u>baking bread</u>.

baker / bake bread

Note: What do you do? = What is your job?

Practice the conversation again. This time use the photos below.

1. painter / paint houses   2. firefighter / put out fires   3. taxi driver / drive a taxi

**GRAMMAR
CHECK**

Simple present vs. present continuous

	Simple Present	Present Continuous
Statements	You **work** in a supermarket. He **studies** English every day.	You **are working** in a supermarket. He **is studying** English now.
Questions	**Do** you **work** in a supermarket? **Does** he **study** English?	**Are** you **working** in a supermarket? **Is** he **studying** English?

Check Points:

✓ Answer present tense questions with *do/does:*
Do you work? Yes, I **do**. / No, I **don't**.

✓ Answer present continuous questions with *am/is/are:*
Are you **working?** Yes, I **am**. / No, I**'m not**.

Listen Listen to each sentence. Is the sentence about something that happens every day or something happening now? Circle *every day* or *now*.

1. every day
   now

2. every day
   now

3. every day
   now

4. every day
   now

5. every day
   now

6. every day
   now

7. every day
   now

8. every day
   now

Sarah's Workday Schedule

10:30:	Arrive at work	2:00–2:30:	Eat lunch
10:45–11:00:	Set the tables	2:30–3:00:	Clean tables
11:00–11:30:	Wash and cut vegetables	3:00–5:00:	Prepare for dinner
11:30–2:00:	Take orders and serve food	5:00–9:00:	Take orders and serve food

---

3 **Pair Practice** Work with a partner. Ask and answer questions about Sarah's workday schedule. Student 1: Ask what Sarah does every day at a certain time. Student 2: Tell a time and ask what Sarah is doing at that moment.

Example: *Student 1:* What does Sarah do at 3:00?
Student 2: She prepares for dinner.
Student 2: It's 3:15 now. What is Sarah doing?
Student 1: She's preparing for dinner.

4 **Pair Practice** Look at the sentences with your partner. Then choose and circle the correct verb.

1. We (start) (are starting) work at 6:00 every morning.

2. The waiter (serves) (is serving) lunch now.

3. They (wash) (are washing) the dishes every afternoon.

4. It's 5:00. He (leaves) (is leaving) his office.

5. I (work) (am working) five days a week.

6. Right now the housekeeper (sweeps) (is sweeping) the floor.

7. They (sell) (are selling) shoes at the department store every weekend.

8. You (fix) (are fixing) the car now.

Write Finish each sentence with one of the phrases in the box.

makes bread	~~helps sick people~~	works in a bank	protects the community
delivers mail	cuts hair	serves food	fixes things

1. A doctor <u>helps sick people</u>   .

2. A waiter   .

3. A mechanic   .

4. A baker   .

5. A mail carrier   .

6. A teller   .

7. A hairstylist   .

8. A police officer   .

6 **Say It** Practice the conversation with a partner.

answer the phone?

A: Is <u>she</u> <u>answering the phone</u>?

B: Yes, <u>she</u> is.

A: Does <u>she</u> <u>answer the phone</u> every day at work?

B: Yes, <u>she</u> does.

Practice the conversation again. This time use the photos below.

1. fix computers?

2. build something?

3. cut hair?

7 Write Write the short answers.

1. Does he work at the clinic?   Yes, _he does_ .
2. Am I washing a car?   Yes, _____ .
3. Are we selling shoes?   No, _____ .
4. Do they work at Burger World?   No, _____ .
5. Are you painting the house?   Yes, _____ .
6. Do you cut hair?   No, _____ .
7. Does she drive a taxi?   Yes, _____ .
8. Are we working at the supermarket?   Yes, _____ .

8 Group Practice Write the name of a job and a place of work on a piece of paper. (Example: cook/restaurant) Don't let other students see it. Pretend this is your job. Walk around the class and ask *yes/no* questions to try to guess the job and workplace of the other students.

Example: *Student 1:* Do you work in an office?
              Student 2: Yes, I do.
              Student 1: Are you a receptionist?

9 Teamwork Task Work in teams of three or four. Look at Angela's neighborhood on pages 102–103. Make a list of the places you see. Then make a list of the workers that work in each place.

PLACE	JOBS
café	waiter, cook, cashier
_____	_____
_____	_____
_____	_____
_____	_____

Homework

Choose a street in your neighborhood. Write a list of the shops and businesses on this street. Then write at least one kind of worker that works in each place. Bring your list to class.

1 Listen and Read Listen to the story. Then read the story.

Angela's Neighbors

Angela and her family like their neighborhood. Their street has many shops and their neighbors are very friendly. Their neighbors are from many different countries and they have many different jobs. Some work in the neighborhood.

Angela's neighbor, Tania, works in the hair salon. She washes, cuts, and styles hair. In fact, she is cutting Hector's hair right now. George and Sarah Chung work in a restaurant. George is the cook. He prepares and cooks food for lunch and dinner. Sarah is the waitress. She takes orders and serves food. Angela and her family sometimes eat at George and Sarah's restaurant. Angela's neighbor, José, works in the gas station. He fixes cars. He's fixing Angela and Hector's car right now. Angela's friend, Lin Tran, works at the bank. She's a bank teller. Angela is depositing a check at the bank right now.

Angela and her family like their community because they know many of their neighbors. They like seeing their neighbors at the shops and businesses in their town.

2 Read Read the sentences. Circle True or False.

1.	Angela's family likes their neighborhood.	True	False
2.	Hector is cutting Tania's hair now.	True	False
3.	George and Sarah work in a restaurant.	True	False
4.	Sarah is a waitress.	True	False
5.	Angela's family sometimes eats at the restaurant.	True	False
6.	Angela's family is eating at the restaurant now.	True	False
7.	Alex is a bank teller.	True	False
8.	José is a mechanic.	True	False
9.	José fixes Angela and Hector's car every day.	True	False
10.	Angela doesn't know many of her neighbors.	True	False

3 **Best Answer** Bubble the correct answer.   **a**   **b**

1. Where do you work?

   a) I work on the bank.   **b)** I work at the bank.   ○   ●

2. Does she eat lunch in the park?

   a) No, she doesn't.   **b)** No, she isn't.   ○   ○

3. What does he look like?

   a) He's very smart.   **b)** He's tall and thin.   ○   ○

4. What do you do?

   a) Very well, thank you.   **b)** I'm a teacher.   ○   ○

5. Where do you live?

   a) I live on Alan Street.   **b)** I live in Alan Street.   ○   ○

4 **Write** Write the names of the numbered places and people in the picture.

1. <u>parking lot</u>   6. _____

2. _____   7. _____

3. _____   8. _____

4. _____   9. _____

5. _____   10. _____

5 **Pair Practice** Discuss these questions about the neighborhood on page 118 with your partner.

1. Where is the hair salon?
2. Where is the post office?
3. Where is the parking lot?
4. What does the police officer look like?
5. What does the mail carrier look like?
6. What does the mechanic look like?

6 **Write** Write about a friend or neighbor on a piece of paper. What does the person look like? Where does he/she live? Where does he/she work? Write as much as you can about the person.

7 **Write** Fill in the blanks with either the simple present or the present continuous form of the verb in parentheses.

1. They (watch) <u>are watching</u> a movie now.
2. You (live) _____ in my neighborhood.
3. Yuko (drive) _____ to work every day.
4. We (work) _____ at the post office now.
5. The park (open) _____ at 9:00 on Saturday.
6. It's 8:00. They (eat) _____ breakfast.
7. He (bake) _____ bread now.
8. Marco (buy) _____ groceries on the weekend.

INTERNET IDEA

Use the Internet to learn more about your community or town. Use the name of your community or town and your state as your search words. How big is your town? How many people are there in the town? What are the nationalities of the people in your town? Tell your classmates about your town.

Pronunciation /b/ and /p/

A. Listen to the words with the /b/ sound.

bank   block   both   bus   bookstore

B. Listen to the words with the /p/ sound.

police   park   place   please   post office

C. Listen and say each word. Circle the letter each word begins with.

1. b / p   **2.** b / p   **3.** b / p   **4.** b / p   **5.** b / p

8 Teamwork Task

A. Work in a team of four or five students. Talk with your team about what a perfect neighborhood looks like. What stores or other places are in a perfect neighborhood? Who works there?

B. Draw a map of a perfect neighborhood. Put your house or apartment on the map, and add stores or other places you want in your perfect neighborhood.

C. Work with your team to write a story about your perfect neighborhood. Use prepositions and names of streets.

Example: Our house is on Main Steet. Next to our house is a park. Across the street from the park is . . .

D. Student 1: read your story to the class. Student 2: show your map to your classmates as Student 1 reads the story. Other students: answer questions from the class about your neighborhood.

I can . . .			
• identify neighborhood places.	1	2	3
• describe locations.	1	2	3
• ask for and give directions.	1	2	3
• read and understand maps.	1	2	3
• talk about my neighborhood.	1	2	3
• identify and talk about neighborhood jobs.	1	2	3
• use in, on, and at for place.	1	2	3
• use adjectives to describe people.	1	2	3
• contrast simple present and present continuous tense.	1	2	3

1 = not well   2 = OK   3 = very well

9 Write Write the correct words in the blanks. Use these words: *do, does, what, go, going, getting, has, curly, tall, know.*

Cindy: Hi Rosa. Where are you going?
Rosa: To the supermarket. I (1) _____ there every Saturday morning.

Cindy: We're (2)_____ to the beach.
(3) _____ you want to come?
Rosa: I don't know. I'm really busy.

Rosa: Who else is going?
Cindy: Alberto's friend, David. Do you (4) _____ him?

Rosa: I'm not sure. (5) _____
(6) _____ he look like?
Alberto: He's tall and thin.

Cindy: He (7) _____ long,
(8) _____ brown hair and blue eyes. And he's very (9) _____.

Cindy: There he is now. He's
(10) _____ out of his car.
Rosa: Okay. Maybe I'm not <u>very</u> busy!

10 Group Practice Practice the story with two other students.

....

Chapter 6 Review **121**

Housing

GOALS

GOALS

- ✓ Identify rooms of a home
- ✓ Identify furniture in a home
- ✓ Describe your home
- ✓ Make a budget
- ✓ Understand housing rental ads
- ✓ Fill out a rental application
- ✓ Respond to housing rental ads
- ✓ Talk to real estate agents
- ✓ Use *there is / there are*
- ✓ Ask and answer *How many?* questions
- ✓ Use *can* for possibility

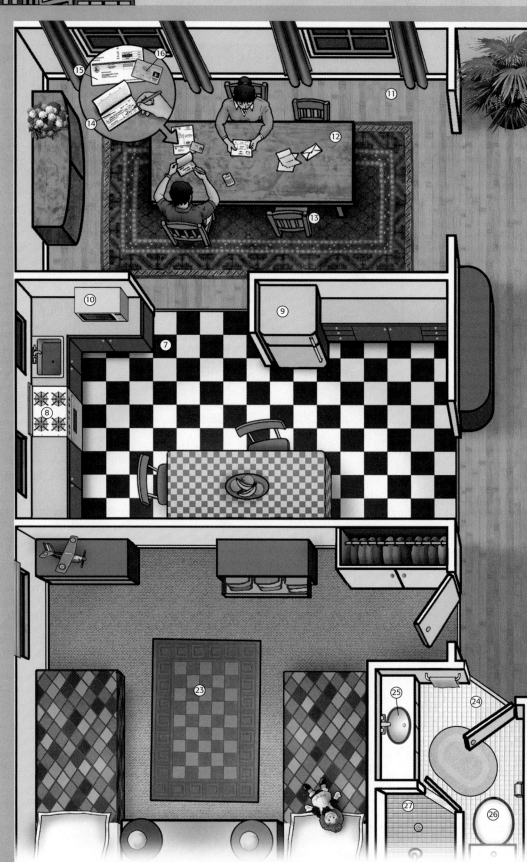

1. living room
2. sofa
3. coffee table
4. lamp
5. television
6. window
7. kitchen
8. stove
9. refrigerator
10. microwave
11. dining room
12. table
13. chair
14. checkbook
15. bill
16. credit card
17. bedroom
18. bed
19. pillow
20. closet
21. mirror
22. dresser
23. rug
24. bathroom
25. sink
26. toilet
27. shower

Angela's Apartment

1 **Write** Which room in your house do you do each of these things in?

1. get dressed _____
2. watch TV _____
3. wash dishes _____
4. sleep _____
5. pay bills _____

6. take a shower _____
7. eat _____
8. relax _____
9. cook dinner _____
10. study English _____

2 **Listen** Listen to the story. Fill in the blanks with the words you hear.

Angela lives in an (1)_____. There are six rooms in the
apartment. There are two (2)_____. The large bedroom is Angela
and Hector's bedroom. Juan and Gloria share the small bedroom. There
is also a small (3)_____. The family watches TV together there.
There is a small (4)_____, too. The family eats together there.
Hector and Angela also pay (5)_____ at the dining room
(6) _____. There is also a small (7)_____ and a small
(8)_____. Angela likes her apartment, but there isn't a lot of
room. She hopes her family can move to a bigger apartment soon.

GRAMMAR CHECK

There is / There are	
There is	***There are***
There is a *chair* in the kitchen.	**There are** *chairs* in the kitchen.
There is a *pillow* on the bed.	**There are** *pillows* on the bed.

3 **Read** Read Activity 2. Underline every *There is* and circle every *There are.*

4 **Write** Look at the picture of Angela's apartment on pages 122–123. Write about some of the things you see in Angela's home.

1. There is a _____ refrigerator _____ in Angela's kitchen.

2. There are _____ in Angela's living room.

3. _____ in Angela's bathroom.

4. _____ in Angela's dining room.

5. _____ in Angela's living room.

6. _____ in Juan and Gloria's bedroom.

5 **Pair Practice** Study the picture of Angela's apartment with your partner for a few minutes. Then close your books and take out a piece of paper. Write a list of as many things as you can remember in Angela's apartment. Use *There is / There are*.

Example: There is a rug in Angela's living room.

6 **Say It** Practice the conversation with a partner.

living room

A: Is there a <u>television</u> in Angela's <u>living room</u>?

B: Yes, there is.

A: Is there a <u>television</u> in your <u>living room</u>?

B: Yes, there is. (or No, there isn't.)

Practice the conversation again. This time use the photos below.

1. kitchen   **2. bedroom**   **3. bathroom**   **4. living room**

Is there / Are there questions and short answers

Is there / Are there questions	Yes	No
Is there a *TV* in the room?	Yes, **there is.**	No, **there isn't.**
Are there *TVs* in the room?	Yes, **there are**	No, **there aren't.**

Check Point:
✓ Use *Is there* with singular nouns and *Are there* with plural nouns.

7 **Write** Write *Is there / Are there* questions with the words below.

1. a mirror / your / bedroom — <u>Is there a mirror in your bedroom</u> ?
2. pillows / your / bed — _____ ?
3. a table / your / kitchen — _____ ?
4. chairs / your / living room — _____ ?
5. a shower / your / bathroom — _____ ?
6. a microwave / your / kitchen — _____ ?

8 **Pair Practice** Ask your partner the questions in Activity 7 about his/her own home.

9 **Pair Practice** Ask your partner *Is there / Are there* questions about his or her living room. Your partner will describe his/her living room to you.

Example: Student 1: Is there a coffee table in your living room?
Student 2: Yes, there is. The coffee table is in front of the sofa.

Try to draw your partner's living room as he/she describes it. Don't show your partner your drawing until you are finished.

10 **Group Practice** Walk around the classroom and ask your classmates *Is there / Are there* questions about the things below. If a classmate says *yes* to a question write his/her name next to the question. Then try to find a student who says *yes* to your next question.

IS THERE / ARE THERE . . .   **WHO?**

1. children in your home?   _____

2. a computer in your home?   _____

3. windows in your bathroom?   _____

4. a cat in your home?   _____

5. chairs in your kitchen?   _____

6. a mirror in your bedroom?   _____

7. a television in your bedroom?   _____

8. pillows on your sofa?   _____

9. a park near your home?   _____

10. friendly people in your neighborhood? _____

11 **Say It** Practice the conversation with a partner.

A: Are there <u>lamps</u> in the room?

B: Yes, there are.

A: How many <u>lamps</u> are there in the room?

B: There are <u>three</u> <u>lamps</u> in the room.

Practice the conversation again. This time use the photos below.

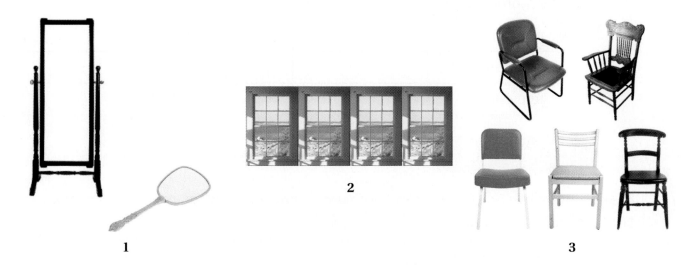

1   2   3

Questions with *How many* and answers

How many	subject	are there	place	Possible Answers
How many	windows	**are there**	in the room?	**There is** one (window/closet) in the room.
				There are two (windows/closets) in the room.
How many	closets	**are there**	in the room?	**There are** no (windows/closets) in the room.

⑫ **Pair Practice** Look at the picture of Angela's apartment on pages 122–123. Ask and answer *How many* questions about the things in the apartment.

Example: *Student 1:* How many windows are there in the living room?
Student 2: There are three windows in the living room.

⑬ **Teamwork Task** Work in teams of four. Interview your teammates about their homes. Ask *How many* questions to complete the chart below.

Name	Student 1 _____	Student 2 _____	Student 3 _____
rooms?			
bedrooms?			
bathrooms?			
people?			
children?			
televisions?			

Game Time

A student will think of a piece of furniture. First, guess what room it is in. Then try to guess what it is.

1 **Say It** Practice the conversation with a partner.

rent?

A: How do you pay <u>your rent</u>?

B: I pay <u>my rent</u> with <u>a check</u>.
How do you pay <u>your rent</u>?

A: I pay <u>my rent</u> with . . .

Practice the conversation again. This time use the pictures below.

1. for groceries?

3. telephone bill?

2. for clothes?

Word Help: Utilities

electricity   gas   telephone

2 **Read** Angela and Hector want a bigger apartment. A bigger apartment will be more expensive. Angela and Hector make a budget to see how much money they can spend on rent each month.

Monthly Budget		
Income: Hector's Salary		$2,000
Expenses: Rent		$1,100
Utilities:		
Electricity		$55
Gas		$40
Telephone		$70
Food/Groceries		$375
TOTAL EXPENSES:		$1,640

$2,000 (Income)
$1,640 (Total expenses)
Extra $360

3 **Group Practice** Discuss these questions about Angela and Hector's budget with your group.

1. What is Hector's income? _____

2. What are their total expenses? _____

3. How much is their rent? _____

4. How much extra money do they have? _____

5. Is it a good idea to spend all the extra money on clothes? Why or why not? _____

4 **Write** Make up a pretend budget for you or someone you know.

Monthly Budget		
INCOME: my salary	_____	
my husband/wife's salary	_____	
EXPENSES: rent	_____	
utilities		
electricity	_____	
gas		
telephone	_____	
food/groceries	_____	
TOTAL EXPENSES:	_____	
_ _ _ _ _ _ _ _ _ _ _ _ _ _ (income)		
_ _ _ _ _ _ _ _ _ _ (total expenses)		
EXTRA: _ _ _ _ _ _ _ _ _		

5 **Problem Solving** Answer the questions.

1. Your weekly salary is $400 a week. Your husband/wife's weekly salary is $275. What is your total monthly income? _____

2. Every week Cindy saves $25. How much will she save in a year? _____

3. Your electricity bill is $45 a month. How much do you spend on electricity in a year? _____

Culture Tip

Credit Card Crazy
Americans use credit cards 200 million times every day.

GRAMMAR CHECK

Can for Possibility		
Subject	***can***	***Verb***
I/You/He/She/It/We/They	**can**	walk to work.

6 **Listen** Angela and Hector want to save money. Listen to them talk about ways they can save money. Check the box next to each way they talk about.

- ☐ Always turn off the lights.
- ☐ Don't make long distance calls.
- ☐ Make long distance calls on the weekends.
- ☐ Make coffee at home.
- ☐ Buy clothes on sale.
- ☐ Use coupons.
- ☐ Walk to work.
- ☐ Buy less food.

7 **Pair Practice** Do you do any of the things in Activity 6 to save money? Talk with your partner about the things you do to save money.

Homework

Before your class meets next, try to save money in different ways. Tell your class about how you saved money and how much you saved.

Apartment for Rent

Word Help: Types of Housing

a single-family home

an apartment

1 **Say It** Practice the conversation with a partner.

DOWNTOWN RENTALS
REAL ESTATE AGENCY
Apartment for Rent
3 bedrooms
Garage
$800/month

A: Downtown Rentals. This is Maria speaking.

B: Hello, Maria. I'm looking for a <u>three-bedroom</u> <u>apartment</u> for rent.

A: I have a nice <u>three-bedroom</u> <u>apartment</u>.

B: Is there <u>a garage</u>?

A: Yes, there is.

B: How much is the rent?

A: The rent is <u>$800</u> a month.

B: Great. I'd like to see it.

Note: A real estate agent is a person who is paid to help people find homes.

Practice the conversation again. This time use the advertisements below.

DOWNTOWN RENTALS
REAL ESTATE AGENCY
Apartment for Rent
1 bedroom
Air conditioning
$850/month

1

DOWNTOWN RENTALS
REAL ESTATE AGENCY
House for Rent
3 bedrooms
Large yard
$1,500/month

2

DOWNTOWN RENTALS
REAL ESTATE AGENCY
Apartment for Rent
2 bedrooms
Dining room
$1,100/month

3

2 **Listen** Listen and check what each caller wants.

CALLER 1	CALLER 2	CALLER 3
☐ a house	☐ a house	☐ an apartment
☐ an apartment	☐ an apartment	☐ a house
☐ two bedrooms	☐ one bedroom	☐ two bedrooms
☐ three bedrooms	☐ three bedrooms	☐ one bedroom
☐ a dining room	☐ near a park	☐ a small bedroom
☐ a garage	☐ near transportation	☐ a small bathroom

3 **Group Practice** Classified ads use many abbreviations. Work in groups of three or four to match the words in the box to the abbreviations below.

~~apartment~~	living room	utilities	yard
dining room	near	bedroom	month
deposit	kitchen	air conditioning	garage

1. apt _____apartment_____
2. BR _____
3. kit _____
4. utls _____
5. gar _____
6. LR _____

7. DR _____
8. mo _____
9. a/c _____
10. dep _____
11. yd _____
12. nr _____

4 ✏️ **Write** Write the ads without abbreviations.

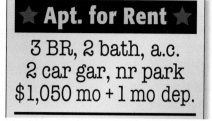

A

Apartment for rent

_____

_____

_____

B

_____

_____

_____

_____

5 **Pair Practice** Work with a partner. Ask and answer questions about the ads above. Student 1: Ask about ad A. Student 2: Ask about ad B.

Example: *Student 1:* How many bedrooms does the apartment have?

6 ✏️ **Write** Pretend you are a real estate agent. On a piece of paper, write a classified ad for a house or apartment. (Use your own house or apartment).

7 **Pair Practice** Fill in the blanks with a partner. Then practice the conversation with your partner.

apartment	rent	bedroom	is	speaking	it

A: Downtown Rentals. Maria _____.

B: Hello. My name is Hector Domingo. I'm calling about the two-_____ _____ for rent. Is _____ still available?

A: Yes, it _____.

B: I'd like to _____ it.

A: You need to come in and fill out a rental application.

8 **Write** Look at Hector's rental application. Then answer the questions below.

```
╔══════════════════════════════════════════════╗
║            RENTAL APPLICATION                  ║
║  ① Applicant's name:  Hector Domingo           ║
║  ② Phone number:      (888) 555-3412           ║
║  ③ Date of birth:     11/15/66                 ║
║  ④ Address:   215 West Second Street           ║
║                       STREET                    ║
║     ⑤ Los Angeles   California   91345         ║
║              CITY         STATE       ZIP       ║
║  ⑥ Employer/Company name:  Sunshine Bus Co.    ║
║  ⑦ Job:   Bus Driver                           ║
║  ⑧ Bank name: Citywide Bank ⑨                  ║
║                    Bank account # 33098-77     ║
║  ⑩ Applicant's signature: Hector Domingo       ║
║                           Date: ⑪ 5/09/05      ║
╚══════════════════════════════════════════════╝
```

1. On what line should Hector print his name? _____
2. On what line should he write his job title? _____
3. On what line should he write today's date? _____
4. On what line should he sign the application? _____
5. On what line should he write his company's name (his employer)? _____
6. On what line should he write the name of the bank? _____
7. On what line should he write his address and phone number? _____

9 **Teamwork Task** Work in teams of three or four. Look at Angela's apartment on pages 122–123. Choose one student volunteer from your team. Other students ask the volunteer questions about his or her home. Ask about rooms and furniture. Write differences between Angela's home and the volunteer's home.

Example: There are two bedrooms in Angela's home. There is one bedroom in Jose's apartment.

Homework

Look at the rental section of a newspaper. Find an apartment that is good for you and that fits your budget. Bring in the ad and show it to your classmates.

① Listen and Read Listen to the story. Then read the story.

A New Home?

Angela likes her neighborhood, but she doesn't like her apartment anymore. There are only two bedrooms in her apartment. She wants an apartment with three bedrooms. There is one small bathroom in her apartment. She wants an apartment with two bathrooms. There is a small kitchen in her apartment, and it is old. She wants a new kitchen. And she wants a yard.

Angela is looking at the classified section of the newspaper for a new apartment. There are two or three interesting ads. The apartments are very big. Of course, the rents are also very expensive! Maybe Angela's apartment is big enough after all!

② Write Answer the questions about Angela's apartment.

1. Does Angela like her neighborhood? _____

2. Does Angela like her apartment? _____

3. How many bedrooms are there in Angela's apartment? _____

4. How many bedrooms does Angela want? _____

5. Is there a kitchen in Angela's apartment? _____

6. Does Angela want a new apartment? _____

7. What is Angela doing now? _____

8. Are the apartments in the newspaper expensive? _____

INTERNET IDEA

Find a good apartment on the Internet. Use one or more of these search words: *apartment, find, rental*. Where is the apartment? How many rooms does it have? How much is the rent? Tell your class about the apartment.

③ Best Answer Bubble the correct answer.

a   b

1. What is in the room?
   a) There is chairs in the room.　b) There are chairs in the room.　　○　●

2. Is there a microwave in the kitchen?
   a) No, it isn't.　b) No, there isn't.　　○　○

3. I am renting a new apartment.
   a) How many bedrooms are there?　b) How much bedrooms are there?　　○　○

4. How do you pay your rent?
   a) I pay with a check.　b) Every month.　　○　○

5. How much is the rent?
   a) There are $800 a month.　b) It's $800 a month.　　○　○

④ Pair Practice Work with a partner. Student 1: Look at Picture A on this page. Student 2: Look at Picture B on page 139. There are different things missing in each picture. Ask your partner *Is there / Are there* and *How many* questions to find out what is missing in your picture. Then draw in the missing items.

Example:　*Student 1:* There is a television in my picture. Is there a television in your picture?
　　　　　　Student 2: No, there isn't. Is the television across from the sofa?

Picture A

Picture B

5 **Write** Write the words for the numbered items in the picture.

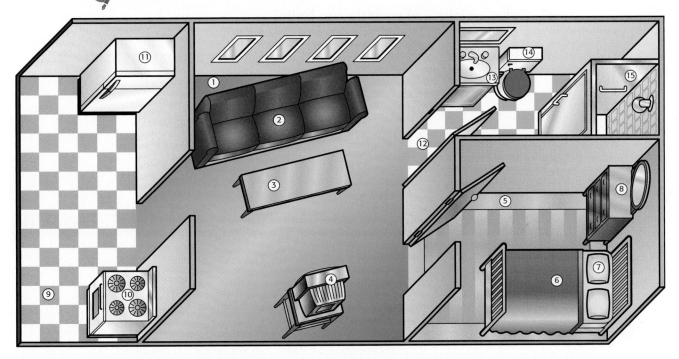

1. <u>living room</u>

2. _____

3. _____

4. _____

5. _____

6. _____

7. _____

8. _____

9. _____

10. _____

11. _____

12. _____

13. _____

14. _____

15. _____

Pronunciation: *sh* and *ch*

A. Listen to the words with the *sh* sound. Repeat the words.

    shower   share   shoes   wash   dish

B. Listen to the words with the *ch* sound. Repeat the words.

    chair   watch   choose   check   itch

C. Listen and circle the word you hear.

    share / chair   shoes / choose   wash / watch   dish / ditch

6 Teamwork Task

A. Work in teams of four or five. With your team, talk about what a "dream house" would look like. How many bedrooms do you want in your dream house? How many bathrooms? What else do you want in your dream house?

B. Write an ad for your dream house. Write as much information as you can.

C. Draw a picture of your dream house.

D. Show the class your picture and tell the class about your team's dream house.

I can . . .			
• identify rooms of a home.	1	2	3
• identify furniture in a home.	1	2	3
• describe my home.	1	2	3
• make a monthly budget.	1	2	3
• understand housing rental ads.	1	2	3
• fill out a rental application.	1	2	3
• respond to housing rental ads.	1	2	3
• talk to real estate agents.	1	2	3
• use *there is / there are*.	1	2	3
• ask and answer *How many* questions.	1	2	3
• use *can* for possibility.	1	2	3

    1 = not well   2 = OK   3 = very well

DOWNTOWN

7 **Write** Write the correct words in the blanks. Use these words: *apartment, available, bedroom, kitchen, garage, there is, There are, How many, Is there, application.*

Cindy: Hi Alberto. What are you doing?
Alberto: I'm looking for a new
(1)_____. My place is too small.

Alberto: This one sounds good. It's a large
one- (2)_____ with a new (3)_____.
Cindy: How much is it?
Alberto: Don't worry. It's not too much.

Alberto: It's a nice neighborhood. And it
has a (4)_____.
Cindy: And a yard too.

Alberto: I'm looking for a one-bedroom
apartment. Is the one in this building
still (5)_____?
Manager: Yes, it is. Do you want to see it?
Cindy: Yes, please.

Manager: Do you have any more questions?
Alberto: Yes. (6)_____ parking spaces
are there in the garage?
Manager: (7)_____ two parking
spaces. Why? How many cars do you have?
Alberto: Just one.

Cindy: (8)_____ a swimming pool?
Manager: Yes, (9)_____. Would you like
to fill out a rental (10)_____?
Alberto: Yes, I would.

8 **Group Practice** Work in groups of three. Practice the story.

Health and Safety

GOALS

- ✓ Identify parts of the body
- ✓ Talk about common health problems
- ✓ Interpret medicine labels
- ✓ Make a doctor's appointment
- ✓ Follow instructions at a medical exam
- ✓ Read a thermometer
- ✓ Call in sick for work
- ✓ Ask for and give advice
- ✓ Identify health and safety workers
- ✓ Report an emergency
- ✓ Use *should*
- ✓ Use *can* for permission

STAY
HEALTHY
•
EAT 5 FRUITS
AND
VEGETABLES
A DAY.

Listen 🎧

Listen and point to the words you hear. Then point to each item in the picture. Listen again and repeat each word.

1. receptionist
2. cough
3. medicine
4. sore throat
5. sneeze
6. backache
7. headache
8. nurse
9. shoulder(s)
10. foot (feet)
11. chest
12. arm(s)
13. head
14. back
15. leg(s)
16. hand(s)
17. stomach
18. doctor
19. patient
20. thermometer
21. eye(s)
22. nose
23. mouth
24. throat
25. tooth (teeth)
26. ear(s)
27. tongue

143

What's the Matter?

Lesson 1

1 Say It Practice the conversation with a partner.

A: Are you OK?

B: No, I'm not so good.

A: What's the matter?

B: My <u>head</u> hurts.

A: Oh, I'm sorry to hear that.

Practice the conversation again. This time use the photos below.

1

2

3

2 Write What problem does each person have? Write these words on the lines: *headache, backache, sore throat, stomachache.*

My head hurts.

My stomach hurts.

My back hurts.

My throat hurts.

1. _____ 2. _____ 3. _____ 4. _____

3 **Say It** Practice the conversation with a partner.

the flu

A: Hello. This is <u>Hector Domingo</u>. I can't come in to work today.

B: What's the matter?

A: I have <u>the flu</u>.

B: OK. I hope you feel better soon.

A: Thank you.

Practice the conversation again. This time use the pictures below.

1. **Lin Tran /**
   a bad cold

2. **Carmen Diaz /**
   a bad headache

3. **Alex Marenko /**
   a bad toothache

Word Help: Cold and flu symptoms

a fever

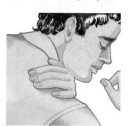

body aches

a runny nose

to cough

to sneeze

the chills

Note: An *absence note* is a note that explains why a child is not in class.

4 Read Gloria has the flu. She can't go to school. Read the absence note that Angela writes to Gloria's teacher. Then answer the questions about the note.

> October 10, 2005
>
> Dear Ms. Gonzalez,
>
>   I am sorry that my daughter, Gloria, can't come to school this week. She has a sore throat and a fever. I think she has the flu. She will be back in class next week, I hope.
>
> Sincerely,
> Angela Domingo

1. What is the date of the note? _____
2. Who can't come to school this week? _____
3. Who is Gloria's teacher? _____
4. What's the matter with Gloria? _____

5 Write On a sheet of paper, write an absence note for your child or a child you know.

Word Help: Fever

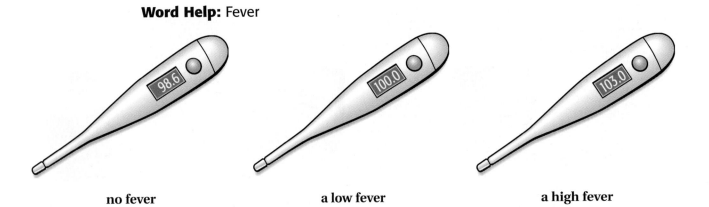

no fever   a low fever   a high fever

6 **Say It** Practice the conversation with a partner.

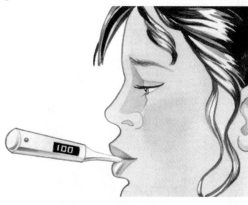

A: Does she have a fever?

B: <u>Yes</u>, she <u>does</u>. She has <u>a low fever</u>.

A: What's her temperature?

B: It's <u>100°</u>.

A: Should we take her to the doctor?

B: Yes, we should. (*or* No, we shouldn't.)

a low fever/100°

Practice the conversation again. This time use the pictures below.

1. no fever / 98.6°   2. a low fever / 99°   3. a high fever / 103°

Culture Tip

Doctor's visits

Colds and the flu are the most common reason people in the U. S. go to the doctor. Back pain is the second most common reason.

GRAMMAR CHECK

Should		
Subject	*should*	*verb*
I/You/He/She/It/We/They	**should**	sleep.
		take an aspirin.

Check Points:
- ✓ Use *should* to give advice or an opinion.
- ✓ Negative form:
  She **should not** sleep.
- ✓ Question form:
  Should she sleep?

7 **Group Practice** Work in groups of three. Look at each of the pictures. Identify the problem. Then discuss the question: What should each person do? Think of as many suggestions as you can.

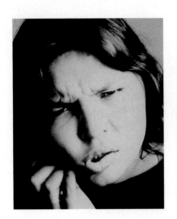

1   2   3   4

8 **Teamwork Task** Work in teams of three or four. With your team make a list of things you should and should not do to stay healthy. Use the words in the box. Then add your own ideas. Write as many things as you can.

| exercise | smoke | sleep | relax | eat sweets | eat vegetables |

WHAT SHOULD YOU DO?

exercise _____

_____

_____

_____

_____

WHAT SHOULDN'T YOU DO?

_____

_____

_____

_____

_____

Game Time

Listen to your teacher's instructions. Only follow instructions when he/she says "Simon Says" first. For example:

Teacher: Simon Says, "Touch your elbow." (The teacher said "Simon Says." So you should touch your elbow!)

Teacher: Touch your head. (The teacher didn't say "Simon Says." Don't touch your head!)

At the Doctor's Office

1 **Say It** Practice the conversation with a partner.

My daughter has a high fever.

A: Good morning. Dr. Casey's office.

B: I need to see the doctor as soon as possible.

A: What's the problem?

B: My daughter has a high fever.

A: The doctor can see her today at 3:00.

B: OK, that's good.

Practice the conversation again. This time use the photos below.

I have the flu.

I have a very bad stomachache.

1   2

2 **Listen** Listen to three people make appointments with a doctor. Write each person's name, the problem, and the day and time of the appointment.

NAME	PROBLEM	APPOINTMENT (DAY / TIME)

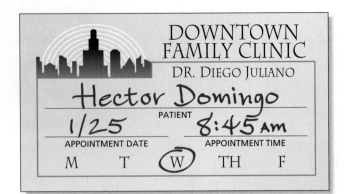

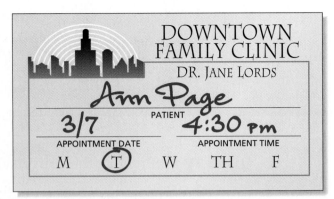

3 **Pair Practice** With your partner, ask and answer these questions about the doctor appointments.

1. Who has an appointment on Wednesday?   _____
2. Who has an appointment in the afternoon?   _____
3. What time is Hector's appointment?   _____
4. What is the date of Hector's appointment?   _____
5. Who has an appointment with Dr. Lords?   _____
6. What day is Ann's appointment?   _____

4 **Pair Practice** With a partner, match the doctor's sentences to the correct pictures.

a. Open your mouth wide.
b. Lift your shirt, please.
c. You should stay in bed.
d. Bring this prescription to a drugstore.
e. Breath deeply, please.
f. Hello. I'm Dr. Grant.

1. __f__

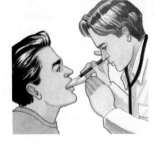

2. _____

3. _____

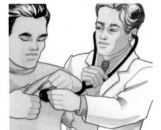

4. _____

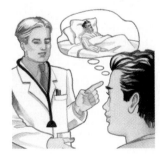

5. _____

6. _____

5 **Read** Read the medicine labels below. Then answer the questions.

Night Time Cough & Cold Formula

Relieves coughing, runny nose & sneezing

DIRECTIONS

Adults and Children over 12: *take 2 teaspoonfuls every 4 hours.*
Children 6–12: *take 1 teaspoonful every 4 hours.*
Not for use by children under 6.

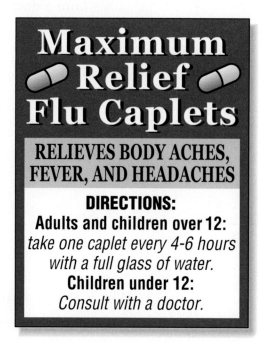

Maximum Relief Flu Caplets

RELIEVES BODY ACHES, FEVER, AND HEADACHES

DIRECTIONS:
Adults and children over 12:
take one caplet every 4-6 hours with a full glass of water.
Children under 12:
Consult with a doctor.

> **Note:** Use *which* to ask a question with a choice between two or more things.

1. Which medicine should you take for a cold? _____
2. Which medicine should you take for a fever? _____
3. Which medicine helps a runny nose? _____
4. Which medicine do you take with water? _____
5. How many Maximum Flu relief caplets should an adult take? How often? _____
6. Juan is 8. How many teaspoons of the Nighttime Cough and Cold Formula should Juan take? How often? _____

> **Note:** Over-the-counter drugs are medicines you can buy at a drugstore without a prescription.

6 **Problem Solving** Answer these questions about the medicine labels.

1. How many teaspoons of the *Night Time Cough and Cold Formula* can adults and children over 12 take in a day? _____

2. How many teaspoons of the *Night Time Cough and Cold Formula* can a 9-year-old child take in a day? _____

3. How many *Maximum Relief Flu Caplets* caplets can an adult take in a day? _____

Note: Prescription drugs are drugs you can only get with a prescription from a doctor.

7 **Read** Read the information on the prescription drug label. Then answer the questions.

PVS PHARMACY
DOCTOR: Dr. Hong Chang
PATIENT: Carmen Diaz
234 Alto Way
Los Angeles, CA
MEDICINE: Amoxicillin
DIRECTIONS: take 2 capsules twice a day
REFILLS: 1   EXPIRATION DATE: 3/29/06

1. Who is the patient? _____

2. Who is the doctor? _____

3. What is the medicine? _____

4. How many pills should the patient take in a day? _____

5. What is the expiration date? _____

6. Can the patient refill the prescription? _____

8 **Teamwork Task** Work in teams of three. Read the health problems. Write what each person should do. Decide if the people should go to work. Write "Yes" or "No."

PROBLEM	ADVICE	GO TO WORK?
1. Alex has a high fever.	He should _____	_____
2. Sarah has a sore throat.	_____	_____
3. Tania has a backache.	_____	_____
4. Carmen has a cold.	_____	_____

Note: Medicine labels can be hard to understand. Ask questions about any directions you don't understand on your medicine labels.

Game Time

One student pretends to have a health problem. The other students guess what the problem is.

Safety Workers

Word Help: Health and safety workers

doctor   nurse   police officer   firefighter   911 operator   lifeguard

1 Write Write one of the jobs from above on each line.

1. _Police officers_____ stop crime.

2. _____ answer emergency phone calls.

3. _____ help patients and doctors.

4. _____ write prescriptions.

5. _____ work at swimming pools and beaches.

6. _____ put out fires.

2 Listen Listen to each conversation. Write the kind of health or safety worker you hear in each conversation.

1. _____   3. _____

2. _____   4. _____

3 **Say It** Practice the conversation with a partner.

A: Can I <u>swim</u> here?

B: No, you can't. The sign says <u>"No swimming."</u>

B: Oh, OK. Thanks.

swim?

Practice the conversation again. This time use the signs below.

1. turn right?

2. smoke?

GRAMMAR CHECK

Can for permission

Subject	*can*	*verb*
I/You/He/She/It/We/They	**can**	smoke here.

Check Point:
- ✓ can not = not have permission
  You **can not** smoke here.
- ✓ can't is the contraction of can not
  You **can't** smoke here.

a fire   a mugging   a car accident

4 **Say It** Practice the conversation with a partner.

A: Hello. 911 operator.

B: I want to report an emergency.

A: What is the emergency?

B: It's <u>a fire</u>.

A: What's the location?

B: <u>235 First Avenue</u>.

Practice the conversation again. This time use the pictures below.

1   2

Note: Dial 911 to report an emergency. Remember, 911 is for emergencies only. Do not call 911 for problems that are not emergencies.

5 **Write** Look at the pictures. Write under each picture: *emergency* or *not emergency.*

1. **a heart attack**

2. **a car accident**

_____

3. **Power outage**

_____

4. **burst pipe**

_____

5. **a person littering**

_____

6. **a robbery**

_____

6 **Pair Practice** Work in pairs. Look at the pictures in Activity 5. Which are emergencies? Role-play a caller calling a 911 operator to report one of the emergencies. Take turns being the operator and the caller. Use the prompts below. Remember, only call about the emergencies!

Student 1: This is 911.

Student 2: _____.

Student 1: What is the emergency?

Student 2: _____.

Student 1: What is the location?

Student 2: _____.

① **Listen and Read** Listen to the story.
Then read the story.

Flu Season at the Domingo House

It is flu season and most of the Domingo family is sick. Juan and Gloria have sore throats. Juan also has a fever. His temperature is 102°. Angela is giving him flu medicine. Gloria's temperature is 98.6°. She doesn't have a fever, but she has a stomachache and a headache. Hector also doesn't feel well. He has chills and body aches. His arms and legs hurt. His shoulders hurt. His back hurts. Even his eyes hurt.

Angela doesn't have a sore throat or a fever. She is the only healthy person in her family, but Angela is tired. She is tired because she is busy helping all the sick people in her family. She should get more sleep. Oh no! Now Angela is sneezing . . . and coughing. Angela is getting sick, too!

② **Write** Answer the questions about the story.

1. Who is sick in the Domingo house at the beginning of the story?

   _____.

2. Who has a sore throat? _____.

3. Does Juan have a fever? _____.

4. What is Juan's temperature? _____.

5. Does Gloria have a fever? _____.

6. What is her temperature? _____.

7. What's wrong with Hector? _____.

8. Why is Angela so tired? _____.

9. Why is Angela sneezing? _____.

10. Who is sick in the Domingo house at the end of the story?

   _____.

3 **Best Answer** Bubble the right answer.   a   b

1. I don't feel very good.

    a) OK.   **b)** What's the matter?   ○   ●

2. I have a bad headache.

    a) You should have the flu. **b)** You should take aspirin.   ○   ○

3. What do police officers do?

    a) They stop crime.   **b)** They help sick people.   ○   ○

4. Can I smoke here?

    a) No, you can.   **b)** No, you can't.   ○   ○

5. Hello. This is the 911 Operator.

    a) My car isn't working. **b)** There is a fire.   ○   ○

4 **Write** Write the words for the numbered items in the picture.

1. <u>headache</u>   6. _____

2. _____   7. _____

3. _____   8. _____

4. _____   9. _____

5. _____   10. _____

5 **Pair Practice** Work with a partner to put the conversation in order. Then practice the conversation with your partner.

____ What's the problem?

____ Can you spell your last name for me please?

__1__ Good morning. Dr. Asim's office.

____ I need to see the doctor as soon as possible.

____ Boris Kosma

____ The doctor can see you today at 3:00.

____ I have a very bad backache.

____ K-O-S-M-A

____ Good. What is your name?

____ OK, I can come in at 3:00.

6 **Group Practice** Work with a group. Discuss each of these situations. What should you or each person do? What shouldn't you or each person do?

1. Your teacher has a very bad cold.

2. Your friend has a backache.

3. You see a man on the street having a heart attack.

4. Your child has a 101° temperature.

5. Your friend is in the ocean, but you can't see her.

INTERNET IDEA

Search the Internet for information about a common health problem like a cold, the flu, a backache, or allergies. What are the symptoms of the health problem? How can you take care of it? Tell your class about the health problem.

7 **Group Practice** Work with a group. Write a list of good reasons to call 911.

_____

_____

_____

_____

PRONUNCIATION Two sounds of *th*

A. *Th* can sound like the *th* in *father*. Listen and repeat the words with this *th* sound.

the   father   that   these

B. *th* can sound like the *th* in *mouth*. Listen and repeat the words with this *th* sound.

thing   health   mouth   thin

C. Listen and mark "X" next to the correct pronunciation of *th* in each word you hear.

th	this	thirty	throat	mother	bath	teeth	then	those
as in fa**th**er	X							
as in mou**th**								

8 **Teamwork Task**

A. Choose an emergency with your team. Make a story about the emergency. What is the emergency? How does it happen? Who does it happen to? Where does it happen? What happens next?

B. You will put on a skit about this emergency with your team. Each member of your team should have a part.

C. Write a script for your skit.

D. Practice the skit with your group. Then perform the skit for your class.

I can . . .			
• identify parts of the body.	1	2	3
• talk about common health problems.	1	2	3
• interpret medicine labels.	1	2	3
• make a doctor's appointment.	1	2	3
• follow instructions at a medical exam.	1	2	3
• read a thermometer.	1	2	3
• call in sick for work.	1	2	3
• ask for and give advice.	1	2	3
• identify health and safety workers.	1	2	3
• report an emergency.	1	2	3
• use should.	1	2	3
• use can for permission.	1	2	3

1 = not well   2 = OK   3 = very well

9 **Write** Write the correct words in the blanks. Use these words: *should, hurts, headache, sore throat, fever, flu, appointment, temperature, matter, not.*

Cindy: Hello, Alberto. Are you okay?
Alberto: No, Cindy. I'm (1)_____ so good.

Cindy: What's the (2)_____?
Alberto: My whole body (3)_____. And I have a (4)_____. And a (5)_____ _____ too.

Cindy: Do you have a (6)_____?
Alberto: Yes, I think so.
Cindy: How high is your (7)_____?
Alberto: I don't know.

Cindy: I think you have the (8)_____. You (9)_____ take some medicine.
Alberto: Mmmmmmm.

Cindy: I need to make an (10)_____ to see the doctor. Today, if possible.

Alberto: Thank you, Cindy.
Cindy: For what?
Alberto: For caring about me.

10 **Pair Practice** Practice the story with a partner.

Food

Listen

Listen and point to the words you hear. Then point to each item in the picture. Listen again and repeat each word.

1. breakfast
2. coffee
3. orange juice
4. pancakes
5. sausage
6. eggs
7. bacon
8. lunch
9. soup
10. sandwich
11. hamburger
12. bun
13. ketchup
14. french fries
15. soda
16. dinner
17. spaghetti
18. milk
19. salad
20. chicken
21. rice
22. dessert
23. cake
24. pie
25. ice cream
26. banana
27. waiter
28. waitress
29. check
30. tip
31. menu

163

Food and Drinks

1 **Write** Look at the foods and drinks on pages 162–163. Write a list of the foods and drinks you like and don't like.

I like . . .	I don't like . . .

2 **Pair Practice** Look at the six food groups. On a piece of paper write the foods from Activity 1 in the correct food group. Then work with your partner to add more foods to each group.

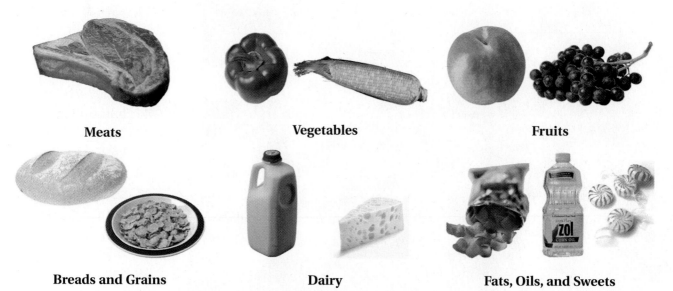

Meats **Vegetables** **Fruits**

Breads and Grains **Dairy** **Fats, Oils, and Sweets**

Note: For a healthy diet, every day you should eat a balanced diet of:
- fruits: 2 to 4 servings
- vegetables: 3 to 5 servings
- breads and grains: 6 to 11 servings
- meat: 2 to 3 servings
- dairy: 2 to 3 servings
- fats, oils, and sweets: very little

3 **Say It** Practice the conversation with a partner.

A: What's your favorite <u>fruit</u>?

B: My favorite <u>fruit</u> is <u>bananas</u>.

A: How often do you eat <u>bananas</u>?

B: I eat <u>bananas</u> <u>once or twice a week</u>.

fruit/bananas/
once or twice a week

Practice the conversation again. This time use the photos below.

1. **meat/chicken/**
   twice a week

2. **vegetable/broccoli/**
   once a week

3. **dairy/cheese/**
   every day

Culture Tip

Most popular fruits

Oranges, apples, and bananas are the most popular fruits in the U.S. What are the most popular fruits in your country?

GRAMMAR CHECK

How often questions and answers

How often	*do/does*			*Example answer*
How often	**do**	I/you/we/they	eat pizza?	I eat pizza **once** a month.
How often	**does**	he/she/it	eat pizza?	He eats pizza **twice** a month.

Check Points:

✓ Answer *How often* questions with *once, twice, three times*, etc.
   I eat pizza **twice** a month.

✓ For a negative answer use *never*:
   I **never** eat pizza.

4 Write Write the answers to the questions.

1. How often do you eat meat?

   _____ .

2. How often do you eat vegetables?

   _____ .

3. How often do you go food shopping?

   _____ .

4. How often do you eat at restaurants?

   _____ .

5. How often do you eat fast food?

   _____ .

GRAMMAR CHECK

Frequency words	
always	100%
usually	
often	
sometimes	
rarely	
never	0%

5 Write Fill in the blanks with the frequency word that is true for you.

In the morning I . . .

1. _____ drink coffee.

2. _____ drink tea.

3. _____ eat cereal.

4. _____ eat eggs.

6 Group Practice Work in a group of three. For each item in the chart, ask each person in your group: *In your family, how often do you _____?* Write the answers in the chart.

Name	do the shopping?	do the cooking?	wash the dishes?

7 **Problem Solving** This bar graph shows the favorite fruits of the students in Angela's class.

Number of students	apples	bananas	oranges	grapes
6				
5		▓		
4		▓		
3	▓	▓	▓	
2	▓	▓	▓	▓
1	▓	▓	▓	▓

1. How many students like apples best? _____

2. How many students like grapes best? _____

3. What is the most popular fruit? _____

4. How many students are in the class? _____

8 **Group Practice** Ask each of your classmates this question: *What is your favorite fruit?* Write each student's name and the name of his or her favorite fruit on a piece of paper.

9 **Teamwork Task** Work in teams of three. Look at your information from Exercise 8. Correct any mistakes. Then use the information to make a bar graph about the favorite fruits of your classmates.

Number of students				
7				
6				
5				
4				
3				
2				
1				

_____   _____   _____   _____

10 **Problem Solving** Answer the questions in Activity 7 about your class.

Homework

Keep a list of what you eat in one day. Look at the note on page 164. Try to eat the right amounts of each food group.

The Supermarket

Culture Tip

Pounds

Most meats, vegetables, and fruits are sold by the pound in the United States. The abbreviation for *pound* is *lb*.

1 Listen Listen and write the names of these vegetables in the picture: *lettuce, corn, tomatoes, potatoes, carrots, onions, mushrooms, broccoli, cucumbers, green beans*

> **Note:** ea. = each
> per = for each

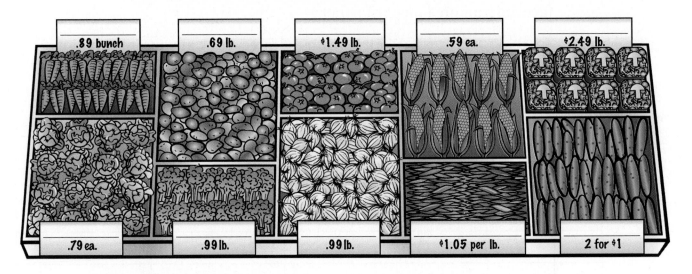

| .89 bunch | .69 lb. | ¢1.49 lb. | .59 ea. | ¢2.49 lb. |
| .79 ea. | .99 lb. | .99 lb. | ¢1.05 per lb. | 2 for ¢1 |

2 Problem Solving Use the vegetables and prices in the picture to answer these questions. Then write more questions. Ask and answer your questions with a partner.

1. How much do three bunches of carrots cost? _____

2. How much do four pounds of onions cost? _____

3. How much do two pounds of mushrooms cost? _____

3 Pair Practice With a partner match the food containers to the foods.

1. a pound of apples

a.

2. a can of soda

b.

d.

3. a bag of potato chips

4. a jar of pickles

5. a box of cereal   c.   e.

4 Write Put the foods in the picture in the correct columns. Then work with a partner to add more foods to the chart.

box	can	bag	jar	pound

5 **Say It** Practice the conversation with a partner.

milk/dairy

A: Excuse me. Where can I find <u>milk</u>?

B: <u>Milk</u> <u>is</u> in the <u>dairy</u> section. That's aisle <u>3</u>.

A: Aisle <u>3</u>?

B: Yes.

A: OK. Thanks.

Practice the conversation again. This time use the pictures below.

1. ice cream/frozen food

2. cakes/bakery

6 **Write** Answer the questions about the supermarket aisles.

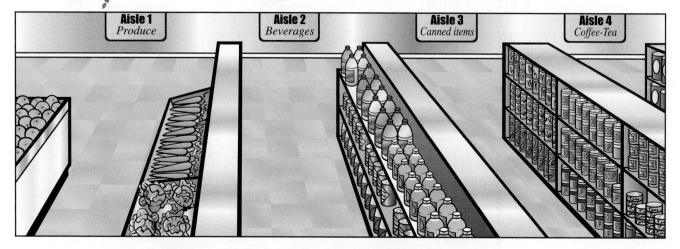

1. What aisle is broccoli in?   _____ .

2. What aisle is soda in?   _____ .

3. What else is in aisle 2?   _____ .

4. What is in the produce aisle?   _____ .

5. What is in the canned food aisle?   _____ .

7 **Say It** Practice the conversation with a partner.

A: I'm going to go to the supermarket this afternoon.

B: What are you going to buy?

A: I'm going to buy <u>tomatoes</u>. They're on sale for <u>99 cents a pound</u>.

Practice the conversation again. This time use the items in the advertisement below.

GRAMMAR CHECK

Future: *Be going to*			
Subject	**be**	**going to**	
I	**am**	**going to**	buy groceries tomorrow.
You/We/They	**are**	**going to**	buy groceries tomorrow.
He/She/It	**is**	**going to**	buy groceries tomorrow.

Check Points:
- ✓ *Be going to* tells about the future.
- ✓ Negative form:
    I am **not going to** buy groceries tomorrow.

8 **Group Practice** Stand in a line with five or six students. Choose a food. The first student in line says: *I'm going to go to the supermarket and I'm going to buy* _____. Then the next student adds a food to the sentence. Continue until the last student speaks. (Try to think of a food that starts with the same letter as your first name!)

Example: Student 1: I'm going to go to the supermarket and I'm going to buy bananas.

Student 2: I'm going to go to the supermarket and I'm going to buy bananas and milk.

9 **Write** Complete the sentences with *be going to* and one of the choices in the box.

eat more carrots and broccoli	pay by check
go shopping this afternoon	order a hamburger
cook at home	have dessert
go on a diet	look at the menu
bring our lunch from home	buy oranges and grapes

1. The school cafeteria is expensive. We _____ .
2. I don't have any cash. I _____ .
3. There is no food in the house. Mom _____ .
4. She likes fruit. She _____ .
5. I don't eat enough vegetables. I _____ .
6. He likes meat. He _____ .
7. I don't know what food the restaurant has. I _____ .
8. You don't want to eat out tonight. You_____ .
9. My pants don't fit. I _____ .
10. She likes sweets. She _____ .

Homework

Go to the supermarket. Make a list of the aisles in the
supermarket. Write the kinds of things you can get in each aisle.

Restaurants

1 **Say It** Practice the conversation with a partner.

A: Are you ready to order?

B: Yes, I am.

A: What would you like?

B: I'd like <u>a cheeseburger</u>.

A: Would you like something to drink?

B: Yes, please. I'd like <u>a glass of milk</u>.

a cheeseburger/a glass of milk

Practice the conversation again. This time use the pictures below.

a bowl of chicken soup / a cup of coffee   **a salad / a cup of tea**   **a pizza / an orange soda**

GRAMMAR CHECK

Would like

Statement:	I **would like** a sandwich.
Question:	**Would** you **like** a sandwich?

Check Points:

✓ *Would like* and *want* mean the same thing. *Would like* is more polite.

✓ Contractions: *I would = I'd, you would = you'd, he would = he'd, she would = she'd, we would = we'd, they would = they'd*

Culture Tip

Where to pay

In casual restaurants in the U. S., the customer pays the cashier. In more expensive restaurants, the customer usually pays the server.

2 **Listen** Listen to each customer's order. Check the boxes next to the foods and drinks you hear.

CUSTOMER 1

☐ cup of chicken soup

☐ fish special

☐ sandwich

☐ tea

☐ bowl of chicken soup

☐ coffee with milk

☐ black coffee

CUSTOMER 2

☐ orange juice

☐ salad

☐ peas

☐ tuna sandwich

☐ apple juice

☐ chicken sandwich

☐ carrots

CUSTOMER 3

☐ pizza

☐ cheeseburger

☐ water

☐ hamburger

☐ coffee

☐ french fries

☐ onions

3 **Pair Practice** Work with a partner. Student 1: Look at Menu A on this page. Student 2: Look at Menu B on page 175. There is different information missing from each menu. Ask your partner questions to find out the missing information on your menu. Then write the information on your menu.

Example: *Student 1:* How much does a chicken sandwich cost?
Student 2: A chicken sandwich costs $4.75.

CHUNG'S CAFE

SANDWICHES AND PIZZA

Pizza	$3.75
Hamburger or cheeseburger	$4.50
Tuna sandwich	$4.75
Chicken sandwich	$4.75

SOUPS AND SALADS

Chicken soup – cup	$
bowl	$2.50
Salad	$3.75

SIDES

	$2.00
Vegetable of the day	$2.25
Rice	$1.50

BEVERAGES

Coffee	$1.00
	$2.25
Milk	$1.25
Soda	$1.50

★ TODAY'S LUNCH SPECIAL
Hamburger & French Fries
$

SANDWICHES AND PIZZA

Pizza	$3.75
	$4.50
Tuna sandwich	$4.75
Chicken sandwich	$

SOUPS AND SALADS

Chicken soup – cup	$1.75
bowl	$
Salad	$3.75

SIDES

French fries	$2.00
Vegetable of the day	$2.25
Rice	$

BEVERAGES

Coffee	$
Orange juice	$2.25
	$1.25
Soda	$1.50

CHUNG'S CAFE

TODAY'S LUNCH SPECIAL

Hamburger & French Fries

$5.50

Culture Tip

Tipping

In the United States, people leave a tip for the server. Tips are usually between 15% and 20% of the total check. 20% is a large tip. Less than 15% is a small tip.

④ **Problem Solving** Use the menu from Chung's Café to fill in the prices of the items below. Add the total price of each check. Then decide how much tip to leave for each check.

CHUNG'S CAFE

Tuna Sandwich	$4.75
Orange juice	$2.25
Coffee	$1.00
TOTAL	

CHUNG'S CAFE

Salad	$
Pizza	$
Soda	$
TOTAL	

CHUNG'S CAFE

Cup of soup	$
Lunch special	$
Milk	$
TOTAL	

1. Tip $ _____

2. Tip $ _____

3. Tip $ _____

⑤ Teamwork Task Work in teams of four or five. If possible, work with teammates from different countries. Complete the chart with popular food and drinks from different countries. List as many countries as you can.

Country	Popular Food	Popular Drink

Note: Ingredients are the different foods in a dish. For example, some of the ingredients of pizza are tomatoes, cheese, and dough.

⑥ Pair Practice Ask your partner about a popular dish (a cooked food) in his/her country. Ask your partner to tell you the ingredients of the dish. Write down the ingredients.

A popular dish in my partner's country is _____

The ingredients of this dish are _____

_____

_____

Game Time

Every student brings a fruit or a vegetable to class. Blindfold a volunteer and put one of the fruits or vegetables in the volunteer's hands. Let the volunteer guess the fruit or vegetable.

Review

1 **Listen and Read** Listen to the story. Read the story.

The Downtown Café

When they go out to dinner, Angela and her family usually go to the Downtown Café. It is close to their apartment and the food is always good. They go there about twice a month. Sometimes they go on Saturday because they have Italian specialties on Saturday and Hector likes Italian food a lot.

Hector always drinks coffee. He likes the coffee at the Downtown Café a lot. The kids usually eat spaghetti. They like to drink soda, but Angela never orders soda for them. She usually orders juice for them.

Angela likes everything on the Downtown Café menu. She sometimes orders chicken and she sometimes orders fish. But she always orders dessert. She loves the desserts at the Café. In fact, she would like to have one right now.

Next Sunday they are going to the Downtown Café again. Angela already knows what she is going to have for dessert. She is going to have the chocolate cream pie. And it is going to be delicious!

2 **Write** Answer the questions.

1. Why does Angela like the Downtown Café? _____

2. How often does Angela's family go to the Downtown Café?

   _____

3. Why do they go there on Saturdays? _____

4. What does Hector like to eat? _____

5. How often does Hector drink coffee at the Downtown Café?

   _____

6. What do the kids usually eat? _____

7. What drink does Angela order for the kids? _____

8. What does Angela want right now? _____

9. How often does Angela have dessert? _____

10. When are they going to the Downtown Café again? _____

❸ Best Answer Bubble the correct answer.

                                                      a   **b**

1. Where can I find milk?
   a) In the dairy aisle.   **b)** Yes, you can.   ● ○

2. How often do you go shopping?
   a) Next Sunday.   **b)** Once a week.   ○ ○

3. What would you like for dessert?
   a) I'd like cake.   **b)** I like cake.   ○ ○

4. What are you going to do tonight?
   a) I go to a restaurant.   **b)** I'm going to go to a
                                        restaurant.   ○ ○

5. How much are the bananas?
   a) They're expensive.   **b)** They're $2.00 a pound.   ○ ○

❹ Write Write the words for the numbered items in the picture.

1. milk
2.
3.
4.
5.
6.
7.
8.

5 **Write** When are you going to go to the supermarket next? What are you going to buy? Write a list on a piece of paper.

 Internet Idea Search the Internet for a recipe you would like to make. Use *recipe* as your search word. Also type in the kind of food you want to cook (for example, *pizza* or *fried chicken*). Tell your class the ingredients and explain how to cook the food. Or make the food at home and bring it in the next day for the class to try!

6 **Write** Write the container and the food.

1. _____

2. _____

3. _____

4. _____

5. _____

6. _____

7 **Pair Practice** With a partner, put the following sentences in order.

____ The customer pays the check.

____ The customer orders.

____ The server brings menus.

____ The customer eats.

____ The server brings the food.

____ The customer leaves a tip.

____ The customer gets a check.

____ The customer sits down.

Pronunciation: Long *e* and short *e*

Listen to the sound of *e* in each word and repeat the words. Circle the words with the short *e* sound (as in <u>e</u>gg) and underline the words with the long *e* sound (as in b<u>ea</u>ns).

ketchup   beef   coffee   tea   menu   check

8   Teamwork Task Work in teams of four or five. Work together to create a restaurant:

A. What are you going to name your restaurant? What foods are you going to serve at the restaurant? Each team member should suggest a food from his or her own country.

B. Write a menu for your restaurant. Write the names of the foods and the prices.

C. Perform a scene in a restaurant. One student is the server. The other students are customers. The customers order from the menus. The server must add up the check. Then the customers must decide on the tip.

I can...			
• identify food and drinks.	1	2	3
• understand food groups.	1	2	3
• read and create a bar graph.	1	2	3
• order food at a restaurant.	1	2	3
• identify supermarket aisles.	1	2	3
• identify food containers.	1	2	3
• read a menu.	1	2	3
• read a check and calculate tips.	1	2	3
• ask *How often* questions.	1	2	3
• use frequency words.	1	2	3
• use *be going to* for the future.	1	2	3
• use *would like*.	1	2	3

1 = not well   2 = OK   3 = very well

Alberto: What (1)_____ you like to drink?

Cindy: Well, I (2)_____ drink juice, but I like tea, too.

Waiter: (3)_____ you like something to drink?

Alberto: We'd (4)_____ a pot of tea for two, please.

Alberto: Do you like (5)_____ ?

Cindy: Yes, I do. Very much.

Alberto: Let's get the fish dinner for two. It's delicious.

Alberto: How about (6)_____ ?

Cindy: Let's get some (7)_____ , with ice cream.

Alberto: Great idea!

Cindy: He's (8)_____ to Mexico next month. He (9)_____ me to go with him to meet his parents.

Rosa: Wow, Cindy!

Rosa: What (10)_____ you going to do?

Cindy: I don't know, Rosa. What should I do?

10 **Group Practice** Work in groups of four. Practice the story.

Work

GOALS

- ✓ Talk about present and past jobs
- ✓ Talk about job skills
- ✓ Understand "Help Wanted" ads
- ✓ Respond to "Help Wanted" ads
- ✓ Fill out a job application
- ✓ Talk about what to do at job interviews
- ✓ Practice interviewing for a job
- ✓ Use *can* for ability
- ✓ Use object pronouns
- ✓ Use the past tense of *be*

PT Receptionist
Downtown Computer Store
M-F, 9:00 - 2:00, $9.00 per hr
Some exp. nec., apply in p
45 Gordon St.

POSITION	EMPLOYER	FROM	TO
Office assistant	ILM Energy Company	1989	1993
Receptionist	Dr.Antonia Ramirez	1987	1989

Listen

Listen and point to the words you hear. Then point to each item in the picture. Listen again and repeat each word.

1. newspaper
2. "Help Wanted" section
3. advertisement
4. pay
5. interview
6. handshake
7. interviewer
8. application
9. experience
10. skills

Jobs

1 **Pair Practice** Work with a partner to unscramble the letters to spell a job. The jobs are *doctor, teacher, waiter, cashier, cook, librarian.*

1. rtdooc   <u>   doctor   </u>   4. kcoo   <u>   </u>

2. iwrtae   <u>   </u>   5. lbraianri   <u>   </u>

3. aheterc   <u>   </u>   6. csahrie   <u>   </u>

2 **Group Practice** What other jobs can you think of? Work with your group to write a list of jobs on a piece of paper. Write as many jobs as you can. Then read your list to the class.

3 **Say It** Practice the conversation with a partner.

now

waitress

three years ago

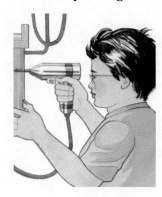

factory worker

A: What's <u>her</u> job?

B: <u>She's</u> a <u>waitress</u>.

A: Was <u>she</u> <u>a</u> <u>waitress</u> three years ago?

B: No, <u>she</u> wasn't. <u>She</u> was <u>a factory worker</u>.

Practice the conversation again. This time use the pictures below.

now   **three years ago**   **now**   **three years ago**

bus driver   **airport shuttle bus driver**   **homemaker**   **receptionist**

Be: Past tense

Subject	be	
I/He/She/It	**was**	in Colombia last year.
You/We/They	**were**	in Colombia last year.

Check Points:

✓ Negative form:

I **was not** in Colombia last year.

You **were not** in Colombia last year.

✓ Negative Contractions:

I **wasn't** in Colombia last year.

You **weren't** in Colombia last year.

✓ Question form:

Were you in Colombia last year?

4 Write Change these present tense statements to past tense statements.

1. The doctor is in the hospital. _____ .

2. I am a nurse in my country. _____ .

3. They are ESL teachers. _____ .

4. The office is open. _____ .

5. We are taxi drivers. _____ .

6. He is happy with his job. _____ .

7. They are at the office every day. _____ .

8. She is a good manager. _____ .

9. You are always on time for work. _____ .

10. We are at the office every day. _____ .

Culture Tip

Changing jobs

On average, people in the U.S. change jobs nine times in their lives.

⑤ Say It Practice the conversation with a partner.

A: What was <u>her</u> last job?

B: <u>She</u> was a <u>waitress</u> at <u>her</u> last job.

A: Really? When was <u>she</u> a <u>waitress</u>?

B: <u>She</u> was a <u>waitress</u> from <u>2001</u> to <u>2003</u>.

waitress/2001–2003

Practice the conversation again. This time use the photos below.

1. florist/2002–2004

2. photographer/1998–2006

3. security guard/2000–2001

⑥ Write Answer the questions about your job experience.

1. Do you work now? _____ .

2. What is your job? _____ .

3. What was your last job? _____ .

4. When were you
   a(n) _____? _____ .

⑦ Pair Practice Ask your partner the questions in Activity 6. Then tell the class about your partner.

> **Note:** Use *can* to talk about ability.
> **Example:** *She can speak three languages.*

8 **Write** Different skills are important for different jobs. Match the jobs with the skills.

JOBS

1. bank tellers
2. 911 operators
3. construction workers
4. homemakers
5. mechanics
6. doctors
7. salespeople
8. lifeguards

SKILLS

a. _____ can answer emergency calls
b. _____ can swim
c. _____ can take care of a home and family
d. _____ can help sick people
e. _____ can build things
f. _____ can count money
g. _____ can fix things
h. _____ can sell things

9 **Write** Write a sentence about the skills needed for each of these jobs.

1. plumber

2. receptionist

3. cashier

4. hair stylist

1. _A plumber can_ _____ .
2. _____ .
3. _____ .
4. _____ .

10 **Pair Practice** What skills do you have? Wite *yes* for each skill you have and *no* for each skill you don't have. Then ask your partner about his or her skills. Write *yes* or *no* about your partner's skills.

CAN YOU . . .	YOU	YOUR PARTNER
1. use a computer?	_____	_____
2. sell things?	_____	_____
3. fix things?	_____	_____
4. take care of children?	_____	_____
5. drive a truck?	_____	_____
6. cook food?	_____	_____
7. use a cash register?	_____	_____
8. paint houses?	_____	_____

11 **Teamwork Task** Work in a team of three or four. Ask your teammates what job skills they have. Make a list of all the job skills of your team. Write as many as you can.

We can . . .

_____

_____

_____

_____

_____

_____

Game Time

Choose a job. Write sentences about what a person with this job can do. Read your sentences to the class. The other students will try to guess your job.

Example: *Student 1:* I can use a hammer. I can climb ladders. I can build things.
Student 2: Are you a construction worker?
Student 1: Yes!

Finding a Job

Note: The part of the newspaper that lists jobs is called the "Help Wanted" section.

1 Pair Practice "Help Wanted" ads use many abbreviations. Work with a partner to match the words and phrases in the box to the abbreviations below.

application	benefits	required	good	Monday to Friday
full-time	necessary	experience	part-time	hour

1. P/T _____

2. M–F _____

3. exp. _____

4. hr. _____

5. nec. _____

6. F/T _____

7. req. _____

8. bnfts. _____

9. appl. _____

10. gd. _____

2 Write Write the ads without abbreviations.

HELP WANTED
COOK
P/T, evenings, $7.00/hr.
no exp. nec.
call for appl. 555-6784

HELP WANTED
SALESPERSON
F/T, M–F, 2 yrs. exp. nec.
gd. bnfts.
call John at 555-6713

COOK

_____
_____
_____
_____

SALESPERSON

_____
_____
_____
_____

3 **Say It** Practice the conversation with a partner.

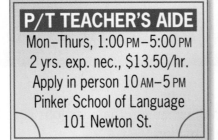

P/T TEACHER'S AIDE
Mon–Thurs, 1:00 PM–5:00 PM
2 yrs. exp. nec., $13.50/hr.
Apply in person 10 AM–5 PM
Pinker School of Language
101 Newton St.

A: What's the job?
B: <u>Teacher's aide</u>.
A: What are the days?
B: <u>Monday to Thursday</u>.
A: What are the hours?
B: <u>1:00 to 5:00</u>.
A: How much is the pay?
B: <u>$13.50</u> an hour.

Practice the conversation again. This time use the ads below.

F/T CASHIER
WANTED
M–F, 8 AM–4 PM
no exp. nec., $8.50/hr
call for appl. (818) 555-3456

TAXI DRIVER
P/T. Sat. & Sun. 6 PM–1 AM
$9.00 per hr. plus tips
No exp. nec.
Apply in person at 656 River Ave.

4 **Teamwork Task** Work in teams of three or four. Look at the ads in Activity 3. Work together to answer the questions about each job. Write *yes* or *no*.

	Teacher's Aide	Cashier	Taxi Driver
need experience?			
full-time?			
part-time?			
apply in person?			

5 Listen Listen to the conversations. Circle the information you hear.

Conversation 1

JOB:	delivery person / doctor
SKILLS:	must be a good swimmer / must be a good driver
EXPERIENCE:	required / not required
F/T or P/T:	full-time / part-time
DAYS:	Wednesday to Sunday / Wednesday to Saturday
HOURS:	6 AM–1:00 PM / 7:00 AM–1:00 PM
PAY:	$13 an hour / $30 an hour
APPLY:	call / apply in person

Conversation 2

JOB:	office assistant / receptionist
F/T or P/T:	full-time / part-time
DAYS:	Monday–Friday / Tuesday–Friday
HOURS:	8:00 AM–3:00 PM / 8:00 AM–4:00 PM
PAY:	$8.15 an hour / $8.50 an hour
EXPERIENCE:	required / not required
SKILLS:	must have good phone skills / must have computer skills
APPLY:	call / apply in person

6 Pair Practice Work with a partner. Practice the conversation.

A: Hello. I'm calling about the cashier job in the newspaper. Is it still open?

B: Yes, it is.

A: I'd like to apply for the job.

B: Do you have any experience?

A: Yes, I do. I was a cashier at the Big Deal Department Store for three years.

B: When were you there?

A: I was there from 1999 to 2002.

B: Would you like to come in and fill out an application?

A: Yes, I would. Where are you located?

Note: Where are you located? = What is your address?

7 **Listen** Listen and circle the word you hear.

1. he / him
2. he / him
3. I / me
4. I / me
5. she / her
6. she / her

Object pronouns

Subject pronouns	Object pronouns	Example sentences
I	me	I call her. She calls **me**.
you	you	You know me. I know **you**.
he	him	He was with you. You were with **him**.
she	her	She works with him. He works with **her**.
it	it	It is empty. We should fill **it**.
we	us	We go with him. He goes with **us**.
they	them	They need us. We need **them**.

8 **Write** Fill in the blanks with the correct object pronouns. (Hint: The underlined words will help you choose the correct object pronouns.)

1. You have <u>an interview</u> tomorrow. You're nervous about _____.

2. <u>Mr. Brown</u> is the receptionist. You should see _____ first.

3. You are going to meet many <u>people</u>. You should shake hands with _____.

4. <u>Ms. Smith</u> is the manager. You are going to have the interview with _____.

5. <u>We</u> like Ms. Smith. She is very nice to _____.

6. <u>Ms. Smith</u> is interested in your experience. You should tell _____ about your last job.

7. <u>You</u> have a lot of experience. I think they are going to offer _____ the job.

8. <u>I</u> can help you get the job. You should listen to _____.

Homework

Read the "Help Wanted" section of a newspaper. Circle a job that sounds good for you. Bring in the ad and show it to your classmates.

Applying for a Job

1 **Group Practice** Work in groups of three or four. Ahmed has a job interview on Monday at 10:30. Write what he *should* or *shouldn't* do for his job interview.

1. He _____should_____ wear clean clothes.
2. He _____ smoke a cigarette at the interview.
3. He _____ wear blue jeans.
4. He _____ shake hands with the interviewer.
5. He _____ introduce himself.
6. He _____ arrive at 10:35.
7. He _____ make eye contact with the interviewer.
8. He _____ talk about his experience.

Culture Tip

Handshake

In the U.S., people shake hands at the beginning and at the end of an interview. Do people shake hands at interviews in your country?

2 **Pair Practice** Ask and answer questions about the statements in Activity 1.

Example: *Student 1:* Should you wear clean clothes at a job interview?
Student 2: Yes, you should.

3 **Teamwork Task** Work in teams of three or four. Make a list of other things you should and shouldn't do at an interview.

YOU SHOULD . . .

_____ .

_____ .

_____ .

_____ .

YOU SHOULDN'T . . .

_____ .

_____ .

_____ .

_____ .

4 Read Ahmed Afar is applying for a job as a manager at a café. Read his application.

COFFEE BEAN CAFE

APPLICATION FOR EMPLOYMENT

Personal Information

NAME: _Afar_____ Ahmed_____ L.____
　　　　Last　　　　　First　　　　　Middle initial

STREET ADDRESS: _1238 Beverly Ave._____

CITY: _Los Angeles_____ STATE: _CA___ ZIP: _90405_

HOME PHONE: _(818) 555-0978_____

SOCIAL SECURITY NUMBER: _134-6X-2121_____

POSITION YOU ARE APPLYING FOR: _Manager_____

Availability

DAYS AVAILABLE:

SUN. ___ MON. X TUES. X WED. X TH. X FRI. X SAT. X

HOURS AVAILABLE: FROM _9 AM___ TO _4 PM___

Work History

POSITION	EMPLOYER	FROM	TO
server	The Tea Leaf Cafe	2002	2005
dishwasher	The Tea Leaf Cafe	2001	2002

5 Pair Practice Ask and answer these questions with your partner.

1. What job is Ahmed applying for? _____
2. What days can he work? _____
3. What hours can he work? _____
4. Does he have experience? _____
5. What was his last job? _____
6. Where was he a waiter? _____
7. What years was he a waiter? _____
8. What was he from 2001 to 2002? _____

Write Fill out this job application with your own information.

COFFEE BEAN CAFE

APPLICATION FOR EMPLOYMENT

Personal Information

NAME: _____

                Last   First   Middle initial

STREET ADDRESS: _____

CITY: _____ STATE: _____ ZIP: _____

HOME PHONE: _____

SOCIAL SECURITY NUMBER: _____

POSITION YOU ARE APPLYING FOR: _____

Availability

DAYS AVAILABLE:

SUN. _____ MON. _____ TUES. _____ WED. _____ TH. _____ FRI. _____ SAT. _____

HOURS AVAILABLE: FROM _____ TO _____

Work History

POSITION	EMPLOYER	FROM	TO

7 Pair Practice Tell your partner about your work experience. Use the information on the application you filled out on page 195.

8 Pair Practice Read the conversation once with your partner. Then practice the conversation again. This time say information that is true about you.

Example: *Student 1:* What was your last job?
Student 2: I was a mechanic.

A: What was your last job?

B: I was a(n) <u>receptionist</u>.

A: Where were you a(n) <u>receptionist</u>?

B: I was a(n) <u>receptionist</u> at a(n) <u>doctor's office</u>.

A: What are your skills?

B: I can <u>use a computer, answer phones, and send faxes</u>.

A: Can you work full time?

B: <u>Yes, I can</u>.

A: We need a(n) <u>receptionist</u> as soon as possible. When can you start?

B: I can start <u>next week</u>.

9 Problem Solving

1. Ahmed has a new job. He earns $10.50 per hour. He works from Monday to Saturday, from 9:00 AM to 4:00 PM
   A. How much does he earn per day? _____
   B. How much does he earn per week? _____

2. Carmen has a new job. She earns $2,000 per month. She works from Monday to Friday, from 7:00 AM to 3:00 PM
   A. How much does she earn each week? _____
   B. What is her hourly pay? _____

Homework

Visit a local business and get an application for a job. Fill in as much of the application as you can. Then bring the application to class. Work on it with your classmates.

---

1 Listen and Read Listen to the story. Then read the story.

Angela's Idea

Angela still wants a new apartment. Hector thinks they don't have enough money, but Angela has an idea. She is going to tell Hector about her idea tonight.

Angela's children are in school now. They don't need her during the day. Angela has time for a job, and she has job skills. She was an office assistant in Mexico. She can use a computer, she can file, and now her English is good enough to answer phones and take messages.

Today there are some interesting "Help Wanted" ads in the newspaper. One ad is for a receptionist job at the Downtown Computer Store. The ad says, "Some experience necessary." It also says "apply in person."

Tomorrow she is going to go to the store and get an application. She is going to tell them about her skills and her work experience in Mexico. Maybe they will hire her, and maybe they won't. But she is going to try.

Angela is excited. This is the start of a new adventure in her new country!

2 Pair Practice Discuss the answers to these questions with your partner.

1. What is Angela's idea? _____

2. Why can Angela get a job now? _____

3. Does she have experience? _____

4. What skills does Angela have? _____

5. What does the ad say? _____

6. What is she going to do tomorrow? _____

7. How does Angela feel? Why? _____

8. Do you think Angela is going to get the job? Why or why not?

_____

3 Best Answer Bubble the correct answer.

a   b

1. Was he a teacher five years ago?
   a) Yes, he were.   b) Yes, he was.   ○ ●

2. Where was she a nurse?
   a) She was a nurse in a clinic. b) She is a nurse in a clinic. ○ ○

3. When was he a cashier?
   a) From 1999 to 2001.   b) Every Saturday.   ○ ○

4. What are her job skills?
   a) She can fix cars.   b) She is fixing a car.   ○ ○

5. What are the hours?
   a) $8.50 per hour.   b) 8:00 AM to 4:00 PM ○ ○

4 Write Write the words for the numbered items in the picture.

1. <u>newspaper</u>

2. _____

3. _____

4. _____

5. _____

6. _____

5 Write Write about your work history on a piece of paper. What was your last job? When were you at this job? Do you have a job now? Are you looking for a job?

Internet Idea
Find a job on the Internet. Use one or more of these search words: *job, find, employment*. Also type in the kind of job you are interested in (for example, *cook* or *nurse*). Where is the job? What are the duties? How much is the pay? Tell your class about the job.

6 Write Write a "Help Wanted" ad for your job or a job you had in the past.

7 Pair Practice Work with a partner to put the sentences of the conversation in order.

_____ **B:** We're at 134 West Main Street. Do you have any experience?

_____ **B:** When were you there?

_____ **B:** Would you like to come in and fill out an application?

_____ **A:** I'd like to apply for the job.

_____ **B:** Yes, it is.

_____ **A:** Yes, I would. Where are you located?

_____ **A:** Yes, I do. I was a cashier at the Big Deal Department Store for three years.

__1__ **A:** Hello. I'm calling about the cashier job in the newspaper. Is it still open?

_____ **A:** I was there from 1999 to 2002.

PRONUNCIATION /s/ and /th/

A. Listen and repeat the pairs of words.

sing / thing	sick / thick	sank / thank
saw / thaw	sigh / thigh	sin / thin

B. Say one word from each of the word pairs in Activity A to a partner. Ask your partner to point to the word you say.

⑧ Teamwork Task

A. With your team, choose a job and make a "Help Wanted" ad for the job. Put this ad on a poster.

B. With your team, write a list of interview questions for this job. Remember to ask about past work experience and skills.

C. Interview students from other teams for this job.

I can . . .			
• talk about present and past jobs.	1	2	3
• talk about job skills.	1	2	3
• understand "Help Wanted" ads.	1	2	3
• respond to "Help Wanted" ads.	1	2	3
• fill out a job application.	1	2	3
• talk about what to do at job interviews.	1	2	3
• practice interviewing for a job.	1	2	3
• use can for ability.	1	2	3
• use object pronouns.	1	2	3
• use the past tense of be.	1	2	3

1 = not well   2 = OK   3 = very well

Rosa: So, where (1)_____ you last night?
Cindy: I (2)_____ with Alberto.

Rosa: And? What happened?
Cindy: He wants to buy plane tickets to Mexico. For both of (3)_____.

Cindy: He called his parents. He told (4)_____ all about me, so now they want to meet me.
Rosa: What are you (5)_____ to do?

Cindy: What do you think I (6)_____ do?
Rosa: I don't know. I think it's a big decision to go to Mexico with (7)_____.

Cindy: He said he can't wait. He wants me to make a decision today.
Rosa: Wow! What are (8)_____ going to tell (9)_____?

Cindy: I'm going to say "yes."
Rosa: You're going to say "yes"?
Cindy: Yes. I'm going to say "yes."
Rosa: (10)_____

10 **Pair Practice** Practice the story with a partner.

Chapter 1: **Personal Information**

Page 3 (Chapter Opening)

Listen *Listen and point to the words you hear. Then point to each item in the picture. Listen again and repeat each word.*

1. form
2. first name
3. last name
4. street
5. city
6. state
7. zip code
8. area code
9. phone number
10. children
11. son
12. daughter
13. mother
14. wife
15. father
16. husband

Page 6 (Lesson 1, Activity 6)

Listen *Listen to the letters of the alphabet. Point to each letter as you hear it. Listen again and repeat each letter.*

a, b, c, d, e, f, g, h, i, j, k, l, m, n, o, p, q, r, s, t, u, v, w, x, y, z

Page 7 (Lesson 1, Activity 9)

Listen *Listen for the correct letters. Complete the names.*

1. Woman: What's your name?
Angela: Angela Domingo.
Woman: Please spell your first name.
Angela: It's Angela. A-N-G-E-L-A
Woman: And your last name?
Woman: Domingo. D-O-M-I-N-G-O
2. Woman 1: What's your first name?
Man 1: Alex. A-L-E-X
Woman 1: And your last name?
Man 1: M-A-R-E-N-K-O
Woman 1: Thank you.
3. Man: What's your name?
Rosa: Rosa Lopez.
Man: How do you spell Rosa?
Rosa: R-O-S-A
Man: Can you spell Lopez too, please?
Rosa: L-O-P-E-Z

Page 8 (Lesson 2, Activity 1)

Listen *Listen and write one of these words under each person in the picture: son, daughter, father, mother, sister, brother, husband, wife, parents, children.*

This is Angela's family:
Ramon is her father.
Anna is her mother.
Ramon and Anna are Angela's parents.
Hector is Angela's husband.
Angela is Hector's wife.
Gloria is Angela's daughter.
Juan is her son.
Gloria and Juan are Angela's children.
Rosa is Angela's sister, and Tomas is her brother.

Page 11 (Lesson 2, Activity 7)

Listen *Listen and circle the words or contractions you hear.*

1. She's my mother.
2. What is your name?
3. You're my friend.
4. They are from Japan.
5. It is a pencil.
6. We're students.
7. I am Chiara.
8. He's my son.

Page 12 (Lesson 3, Activity 1)

Listen *Listen and repeat the numbers.*

zero, one, two, three, four, five, six, seven, eight, nine, ten, eleven, twelve, thirteen, fourteen, fifteen, sixteen, seventeen, eighteen, nineteen, twenty, thirty, forty, fifty, sixty, seventy, eighty, ninety, one hundred

Page 13 (Lesson 3, Activity 4)

Listen *Listen to the addresses. Write the missing numbers.*

1. 26 Clark Street
2. 150 Brown Street
3. 80 East End Avenue
4. Apartment 15
5. 246 River Street
6. 300 Avenue A

Page 16 (Lesson 3, Activity 11)

Listen *Listen and write the missing letters and numbers on the envelope.*

A: I need to address this envelope to Bill Lewis. How do you spell his last name?

B: L – E – W – I – S.
A: And what's his address?
B: One sixty–two Broad Avenue. That's B – R – O – A – D Avenue.
A: What's his city and state?
B: He lives in Austin, Texas.
A: Can you spell the city?
B: A – U – S – T – I - N.
A: And the state?
B: Texas. T – E – X – A - S.
A: What's his zip code?
B: His zip code is 78701.

Page 17 (Chapter Review, Activity 1)

Listen and Read *Listen to the story. Then read the story.*

My Family

My name is Angela Domingo. I'm married. My husband's name is Hector. We're from Mexico, but Los Angeles, California, is our home now.

Our son, Juan, is eight years old. Gloria is our daughter. She's six. Our address is 215 West Second Street. Our telephone number is area code (818) 555-3412.

My sister is in Los Angeles too. Her name is Rosa Lopez. She's single. My brother is here, too. His name is Tomas. He's divorced. My family is happy in Los Angeles.

Page 20 (Chapter Review)

Pronunciation: *Short i and long e*

A. *Listen to the word pairs. The first word has the short i sound (/i/ as in it). The second word has the long e sound (/e/ as in eat).*

1.	is	ease
2.	hit	heat
3.	its	eats
4.	sit	seat
5.	fill	feel
6.	sick	seek
7.	itch	each
8.	live	leave

B. *Listen and circle the word you hear.*

1. is
2. heat
3. eats
4. sit
5. fill
6. sick
7. each
8. leave

Chapter 2: **School**

Page 23 (Chapter Opening)

Listen *Listen and point to the words you hear. Then point to each item in the picture. Listen again and repeat each word.*

1. teacher
2. student
3. desk
4. chair
5. apple
6. notebook
7. pencil
8. eraser
9. board
10. classroom
11. counselor
12. pen
13. umbrella
14. office assistant
15. folder
16. computer
17. office
18. cook
19. cashier
20. cafeteria
21. librarian
22. book
23. library

Page 34 (Lesson 3, Activity 6)

Listen *Listen and circle the worker you hear.*

1. Eric Ryan: Please take out your books and turn to page 35. Angela, please read the story out loud.
2. Woman: The soda is a dollar, the hamburger is $3.25, and the french fries are $1.75. That's six dollars, please.
3. Ann Page: This is a list of the English classes at this school. Take it home and look at it tonight. Then tomorrow we'll talk about the classes.
4. Man: This is a very good book. You can take it home, but bring it back in two weeks. Don't forget!
5. Woman: I'm sorry, Ms. Smith is not in the office today. What is your name? And your telephone number? OK. I'll give Ms. Smith the message.
6. Man: The hamburger is ready, but the french fries are still cooking. What's the next order?

Page 37 (Chapter Review, Activity 1)

Listen and Read *Listen to the story. Then read the story.*

My School

Hi. I'm Angela. I'm a student at the Downtown Adult School. My sister is a student, too, but she isn't in my class. Her class is in Room 25. I'm in Room 33. Room 33 is next to the library and across from the office. I'm in class right now. Lin Tran is in front of me and Marie is behind me. They are both good friends. George Chung is between me and his wife. He isn't in class every day, but he's a good student. All the students in my class are nice people.

The staff at my school is great. Mr. Ryan is my teacher. He's a really good teacher. Carol is the office assistant. She's a hard worker, but she's very friendly. Ann Page is the counselor. Go to her if you have a problem. I'm very happy at the Downtown Adult School because all the people are so helpful and nice.

Page 40 (Chapter Review)

Pronunciation: a and an

A. *We usually pronounce the word* a *like "uh." Listen and repeat.*

a pen
a box
a cook
a teacher
a good student

B. *We pronounce the "a" in* an *with a short a sound. Listen and repeat.*

an apple
an eraser
an umbrella
an office
an adult

Chapter 3: Shopping

Page 43 (Chapter Opening)

Listen *Listen and point to the words you hear. Then point to the part of the picture that shows each word. Listen again and repeat each word.*

1. cashier
2. customer
3. check
4. receipt
5. bills
6. change
7. dress
8. blouse
9. sweater
10. skirt
11. belt
12. jacket
13. shirt
14. pants
15. shoes
16. suit
17. tie
18. salesperson
19. white
20. yellow
21. gray
22. green
23. red
24. orange
25. brown
26. blue
27. black

Page 48 (Lesson 2, Activity 2)

Listen *Listen and write the price you hear.*

1. A: How much is the pen?
B: It's sixty-nine cents.
2. A: How much is that orange T-shirt?
B: It's eight dollars and ninety-five cents.

3. A: I like this tie! How much is it?
B: It's nineteen dollars and ninety-nine cents.
4. A: How much is that great leather jacket?
B: It's one hundred and twenty-five dollars.

Page 53 (Lesson 3, Activity 2)

Listen *Listen to the conversations. Write the kind of clothes, colors, and sizes the people want.*

1. Salesperson: May I help you?
Woman: Yes, please. I'm looking for a red blouse.
Salesperson: What size do you need?
Woman: Small, please.
2. Man: Excuse me. Do you have T-shirts?
Salesperson: What color do you want?
Man: Red.
Salesperson: And what size?
Man: Medium.
3. Man: I'm looking for a brown sweater.
Salesperson: What size do you need?
Man: Do you have extra large?
4. Woman: Excuse me. Does this store have dresses?
Salesperson: What color dress are you looking for?
Woman: Blue.
Woman: And the size?
Salesperson: Large.

Page 57 (Chapter Review, Activity 1)

Listen and Read *Listen to the story. Then read the story.*

Shopping for School

It is September and Angela's children need new clothes for school. Her son, Juan, needs a pair of pants. The department store has a pair of blue pants. Juan really likes them, but they are $50. He doesn't need that pair of pants!

Gloria is Angela's daughter. Gloria likes red clothes. She wants a red skirt, a red shirt, and red shoes. Does Gloria need red clothes? No, she doesn't. Gloria needs a uniform for school. The uniform is a black skirt, white shirt, and brown shoes. The skirt is $25, the shirt is $20, and the shoes are $40.

Angela is going to school, too. She is a student in an English class. Angela needs many things for her class. She needs a notebook, a dictionary, textbooks, and a good pen. Angela needs more money!

Page 59 (Chapter Review, Activity 5)

Listen *Listen to the conversation. Write the prices you hear on the right price tags.*

Man: How much is the tie?
Salesperson: It's fifteen dollars
Man: Hmm. How about the gray pants?
Salesperson: They're twenty-five ninety-five.
Man: What about the leather jacket?
Salesperson: It's eighty-nine ninety-nine.

Woman: How much is the white blouse in the window?

Salesperson: It's twenty-nine ninety-nine.

Woman: And the skirt?

Salesperson: It's on sale for twenty-eight dollars.

Woman: Are the high-heeled shoes on sale too?

Salesperson: No, they're not. The shoes are thirty-five ninety-eight.

Page 59 (Chapter Review)

Pronunciation: /s/ and /z/

A. *Listen for the /s/ sound at the end of each word. Repeat each word.*

pants	socks	belts
checks	skirts	

B. *Listen for the /z/ sound at the end of each word. Repeat each word.*

ties	customers	dollars
bills	shoes	

C. *Listen. Circle the words with the /s/ sound. Underline the words with the /z/ sound.*

shirts	dimes	stores
jackets	suits	

Chapter 4: **Time**

Page 63 (Chapter Opening)

Listen *Listen and point to the words you hear. Then point to each item in the picture. Listen again and repeat each word.*

1. calendar
2. year
3. month
4. date
5. day
6. weekend
7. clock
8. breakfast
9. watch
10. lunch
11. dinner
12. morning
13. afternoon
14. evening

Page 65 (Lesson 1, Activity 3)

Listen and Write *Listen to the conversations. For each conversation, write the time you hear under the clock. Then draw the time on the clock.*

1. Woman: Excuse me. What time do you have?

Man: Two thirty.

Woman: I'm sorry. What time is it?

Man: Two thirty.

2. Woman 1: What time is it now?

Woman 2: It's eight forty-five.

Woman 1: I'm sorry. What?

Woman 2: It's eight forty-five.

3. Man: Excuse me. What time is it?

Woman: Ten thirty.

Man: I'm sorry. Can you repeat that?

Woman: Ten thirty.

4. Man 1: What time do you have?

Man 2: Six twenty.

Man 1: Thanks.

5. Man: What time do you have?

Woman: It's seven twenty-five.

6. Woman: Excuse me. Do you know the time?

Man: It's four fifteen.

7. Woman 1: What time do you have?

Woman 2: It's one forty-five.

8. Man: What time do you have?

Woman: It's six thirty.

Page 66 (Lesson 1, Activity 5)

Listen *Listen to the ordinal numbers. Point to each number as you hear it and repeat the number.*

First, second, third, fourth, fifth, sixth, seventh, eighth, ninth, tenth, eleventh, twelfth, thirteenth, fourteenth, fifteenth, sixteenth, seventeenth, eighteenth, nineteenth, twentieth, twenty-first, twenty-second, twenty-third, twenty-fourth, twenty-fifth, twenty-sixth, twenty-seventh, twenty-eighth, twenty-ninth, thirtieth, thirty-first.

Page 69 (Lesson 2, Activity 1)

Listen and Write *Write the correct verbs under the pictures. Use the verbs in the box. Then listen to Cindy to check your answers.*

Cindy: What do I do every morning? Well, I get up at 6:00. Then at 6:15 I take a shower. At 6:30 I brush my teeth. After that I get dressed. I guess it's about 6:35 when I get dressed.Then I make my bed at about 6:45. And then I eat breakfast at about 7:00. After breakfast, at about 7:15, I wash the dishes. At about 7:20 I study English. I study until about 8:00. Then at 8:00 I go to work.

Page 74 (Lesson 3, Activity 3)

Listen *Listen to Cindy describe her workday. Fill in the times you hear.*

Cindy: OK. Now I'll tell you about my workday. I arrive at the supermarket at 8:15. I check in first in the office. Then at 8:30 I start work in the bakery. I make coffee right away at about 8:35. I make three different kinds of coffee. It only takes about ten minutes. At 8:45 I put out fresh pastries on the shelves. Then I work in the bakery for about three hours, from 9:00 to 12:00. From 12:00 to 1:00 I eat lunch in the break room and talk with my co-workers. Sometimes I read a book. After lunch I usually help out at the deli counter from 1:00 to 3:00. At around 3:00 I clean up the bakery and the deli areas. Then at about 3:30 I sweep the floor of the supermarket. Then at 4:00, I leave work and go to school. I work at the supermarket, but at night I'm studying to be an animal doctor.

Page 77 (Chapter Review, Activity 1)

Listen and Read *Listen to the story. Then read the story.*

Many Kinds of Jobs

My husband, Hector, gets up at six o'clock every morning. He takes a quick shower, brushes his teeth, and gets dressed. He drinks a cup of coffee and goes to work at 6:30. At work, he drives a bus all day.

My sister Rosa gets up at eight o'clock. She takes a long shower. She drinks a cup of tea. Then she rides her bicycle to the park. She doesn't go to work in the morning. She eats lunch at home. Then she goes to work in the afternoon. She is a cashier. She works at the Shop & Save supermarket.

I don't have a job, but I work at home every day. I am a homemaker. Every morning I get up early. I cook breakfast for my children before they go to school. At eight o'clock I take my children to school. In the afternoon I clean our apartment, buy groceries, and study English. I don't work in an office, but I have a full-time job at home!

Page 80 (Chapter Review)

Pronunciation: *Time*

A. *Listen to and repeat each of these times.*

12:15   12:50   8:13   8:30
7:14   7:40

B. *Listen and write the times you hear.*

1.   11:30
2.   2:13
3.   6:40
4.   1:15

Chapter 5: **Busy Lives**

Page 83 (Chapter Opening)

Listen *Listen and point to the words you hear. Then point to the person or animal in the picture doing each action. Listen again and repeat each word.*

1.   cooking
2.   eating
3.   giving
4.   taking
5.   drinking
6.   singing
7.   dancing
8.   listening
9.   sleeping
10.   throwing
11.   jumping
12.   selling
13.   buying
14.   swimming
15.   walking
16.   flying
17.   working

Page 89 (Lesson 2, Activity 2)

Listen *The Domingo family is on vacation. Listen to the different things they are doing on their vacation. Choose one of the words in the box for each activity you hear*

1.   Juan: Dad, Gloria is splashing me.
Hector: Gloria, don't splash your brother.
Gloria: I'm not. He's splashing me!
2.   Angela: I'm looking for a gift to take home.
Shopkeeper: We have nice T-shirts.
Angela: How much are they?
3.   Angela: Ow! You're stepping on my foot.
Hector: Sorry.
4.   Gloria: Mom, Juan is taking my french fries.
Angela: Don't do that Juan. Here Gloria, have my fries. I don't want them.
5.   Hector: I'm tired. I need a rest.
Angela: Already?
Hector: You're going too fast.
6.   Angela: Hector? Hector? Wake up.
Hector: What?
Angela: You're snoring.
Hector: Oh, sorry.

Page 95 (Lesson 3, Activity 6)

Listen and Write *Listen to Irma talk about her job. Write the things that are missing from her work schedule.*

IRMA: I am a housekeeper. I work for the Casey family. Mr. and Mrs. Casey have two little boys. On my workdays I arrive at the Casey house at 7:00. At 7:15 I help the children get dressed.

At 7:30 I cook breakfast. At 7:45 I feed the kids. Then at 7:50 I take the children to school. I get back to the house about 9:00. At 9:00 I wash the dishes. And then I do the laundry at 9:30.

At about 11:30 I usually take a break and relax for an hour. Then, at 12:30 I go to the supermarket and buy groceries. At 1:30 I make lunch. At 2:30 I pick up the kids from school. Then at 3:00 I say goodbye and go home. That's my workday at the Casey house.

Page 97 (Chapter Review, Activity 1)

Listen and Read *Listen to the story. Then read the story.*

A Busy Day

It is three o'clock on Monday afternoon and many things are happening in my neighborhood. Parents are picking up their children from school. People are buying groceries at the supermarket. At the clinic, the doctor and the nurse are helping patients and Carmen is answering the phone.

I'm not working in the clinic or in a restaurant. I am at home, but I'm busy, too. Right now I'm washing the dishes, doing the laundry, and taking care of my kids, all at the same time.

My neighbors, George and Sarah Chung, aren't working in their restaurant today. They're on vacation. They are at the beach right now. Maybe they're swimming. Or maybe they're sitting in the sun and relaxing. I don't know what they're doing, but I'm sure they are busy having a good time!

Page 100 (Chapter Review)

Pronunciation: /j/ and /y/

A. *Listen and repeat the words with the /j/ sound.*

job	jump	jar
jeans	just	

B. *Listen and repeat the words with the /y/ sound.*

you	yellow	young
yes	your	

C. *Listen to the pairs of words. Practice them with a partner.*

jet – yet	jam – yam
jell – yell	jeer – year

Chapter 6: **The Community**

Page 103 (Chapter Opening)

Listen *Listen and point to the words you hear. Then point to each item in the picture. Listen again and repeat each word.*

1. library
2. post office
3. gas station
4. hair salon
5. drugstore
6. clinic
7. parking lot
8. bus station
9. bookstore
10. café
11. apartment building
12. park
13. mail carrier
14. mechanic
15. doctor
16. hairstylist
17. police officer
18. street sign

Page 106 (Lesson 1, Activity 6)

Listen *Look at the map. Listen to the directions. Put the places below in the correct boxes on the map. Write only the first letter of each place in the boxes.*

1. Woman: Excuse me. Where is the bus station?

Man: You need to walk east on 21st Street. Then turn left on Avenue M. The station is between 22nd and 23rd Streets.

Woman: Thanks.

Man: You're welcome.

2. Man 1: Excuse me. I'm looking for the Adult School.

Man 2: Let's see. Go north on Avenue J. When you get to 22nd Street, turn right. Go straight for two blocks. The school is between Avenue L and Avenue M.

Man 1: Thanks.

Man 2: Sure.

3. Man: How can I get to the computer store from here?

Woman: Walk north on Avenue J to 23rd St. Turn right onto 23rd Street. Go 2 blocks to Avenue L. Turn left on Avenue L. The computer store is on the left.

Man: Great. Thanks.

4. Woman 1: Excuse me. I'm looking for the library.

Woman 2: OK. Go north on Avenue J to 24th St. Turn right on 24th Street and walk straight. It's between Avenue K and Avenue L on the right side.

Woman 1: Thank you.

Woman 2: You're welcome.

5. Man 1: How can I get to the park from here?

Man 2: That's easy. Go north on Avenue J to 24th St. Turn right. Go one block to Avenue K. The park is on the corner of 24th Street and Avenue K.

Man 1: OK. Thanks.

Man 2: No problem.

Page 112 (Lesson 2, Activity 5)

Listen *Listen and write one of these names under each person in the picture:* Debbie, Jahmal, Barbara, Hoshi, Rags, Steve.

Woman: So, tell me about your neighbors.

Man: Well, that heavy woman with blond hair is Debbie. She lives right next door to me. She's a teacher. Hoshi is the short woman with the long hair and brown eyes. She lives on the first floor. She's a student and a good friend. And that tall woman over there? The one with the gray hair? That's Barbara. Barbara lives on the second floor with her husband. She's a really nice woman. Jahmal is the heavy man with the dark hair. I think he's a doctor. And you see that very tall man with the long, blonde hair? That's Steve. Steve lives across the hall. He's a nice guy but he plays his music too loud. And the dog with the long hair? That's Steve's dog, Rags.

Page 114 (Lesson 3, Activity 2)

Listen *Listen to each sentence. Is the sentence about something that happens every day or something happening now? Circle* every day *or* now.

1. He works at the post office.
2. She is serving dinner.
3. They are painting a house.
4. You always come to work on time.
5. He works from 8:00 to 5:00.
6. I drive a bus.
7. They're using the computers.
8. We're baking bread.

Page 117 (Chapter Review, Activity 1)

Listen and Read *Listen to the story. Then read the story.*

Angela's Neighbors

Angela and her family like their neighborhood. Their street has many shops and their neighbors are very friendly. Their neighbors are from many different countries and they have many different jobs. Some work in the neighborhood.

Angela's neighbor, Tania, works in the hair salon. She washes, cuts, and styles hair. In fact, she is cutting Hector's hair right now. George and Sarah Chung work in a restaurant. George is the cook. He prepares and cooks food for lunch and dinner. Sarah is the waitress. She takes orders and serves food. Angela and her family sometimes eat in George and Sarah's restaurant. Angela's neighbor, Jose, works in the gas station. He fixes cars. He's fixing Angela and Hector's car right now. Angela's friend, Lin Tran, works at the bank. She's a bank teller. Angela is depositing a check at the bank right now.

Angela and her family like their community because they know many of their neighbors. They like seeing their neighbors at the shops and businesses in their town.

Page 120 (Chapter Review)

Pronunciation: /b/ and /p/

A. *Listen to the words with the /b/ sound.*

bank	block	both
bus	bookstore	

B. *Listen to the words with the /p/ sound.*

police	park	place
please	post office	

C. *Listen and say each word. Circle the letter each word begins with.*

1. pair
2. back
3. bike
4. boss
5. pink

Chapter 7: **Housing**

Page 123 (Chapter Opening)

Listen *Listen and point to the words you hear. Then point to each item in the picture. Listen again and repeat each word.*

1. living room
2. sofa
3. coffee table
4. lamp
5. television
6. window
7. kitchen
8. stove
9. refrigerator
10. microwave
11. dining room
12. table
13. chair
14. checkbook
15. bill
16. credit card
17. bedroom
18. bed
19. pillow
20. lamp
21. closet
22. mirror
23. dresser
24. rug
25. bathroom
26. sink
27. mirror
28. toilet
29. shower

Page 124 (Lesson 1, Activity 2)

Listen *Listen to the story. Fill in the blanks with the words you hear.*

Angela lives in an _____ (1). There are six rooms in the apartment. There are two

_____ (2). The large bedroom is Angela and Hector's bedroom. Juan and Gloria share the small bedroom. There is also a

_____ _____ (3). The family watches TV together there. There is a

small _____ _____ (4), too. The family eats together there. Hector and

Angela also pay _____ (5) at the

dinning room _____ (6). There is

also a small _____ (7) and a small

_____ (8). Angela likes her apartment, but there isn't a lot of room. She hopes her family can move to a bigger apartment soon.

Page 132 (Lesson 2, Activity 6)

Listen *Angela and Hector want to save money. Listen to them talk about ways they can save money. Check the box next to each way they talk about.*

Angela: Can we can rent a bigger apartment? Do we have enough money?

Hector: Well, we have some extra money in our budget, but we need to save some more money.

Angela: How can we save more money?

Hector: Well. . . I buy a cup of coffee every morning. But that's expensive! I can just make coffee at home in the morning. That saves an extra dollar every day.

Angela: Hmm. We spend a lot of money on groceries every week. I can use coupons at the supermarket.

Hector: We also leave the lights on too much. Electricity is expensive. We can turn off the lights every time we leave the house.

Angela: We can call my parents in Mexico on the weekends. Phone calls are cheaper on the weekend.

Hector: Great. There are a lot of ways we can save money.

Page 134 (Lesson 3, Activity 2)

Listen *Listen and check what each caller wants.*

1. Real estate agent: Downtown rentals. Tom speaking. Can I help you?

Woman: Yes. I'd like to know if you have any two-bedroom apartments for rent?

Real estate agent: Yes, we have a very nice two-bedroom apartment for rent.

Woman: Does it have a dining room?

Real Estate Agent: Yes, it does. It also has a large living room.

Woman: That sounds good. When can I see it?

2. Real estate agent: Downtown rentals.This is Maggie.

Man: Hello. I'm looking for a three-bedroom house.

Real Estate agent: Hmmm. We have a three-bedroom house, but it's not in the city.

Man: Is it near public transportation?

Real estate agent: Yes, there's a bus station two blocks away.

Man: Great. I'd like to see the house.

3. Real estate agent: Downtown rentals. Benny here.

Man: Hi. I need to rent an apartment.

Real estate agent: How many bedrooms?

Man: Just one bedroom.

Real estate agent: I have a one-bedroom apartment in the city. But it has a very small bathroom.

Man: That's OK. When can I see the apartment?

Page 137 (Chapter Review, Activity 1)

Listen and Read *Listen to the story. Then read the story.*

A New Home?

Angela likes her neighborhood, but she doesn't like her apartment anymore. There are only two bedrooms in her apartment. She wants an apartment with three bedrooms. There is one small bathroom in her apartment. She wants an apartment with two bathrooms. There is a small

kitchen in her apartment, and it is old. She wants a new kitchen. And she wants a yard.

Angela is looking at the classified section of the newspaper for a new apartment. There are two or three interesting ads. The apartments are very big. Of course the rents are also very expensive! Maybe Angela's apartment is big enough after all!

Page 140 (Chapter Review)

Pronunciation: *sh and ch*

A. *Listen to the words with the sh sound. Repeat the words.*

shower	share	shoes
wash	dish	

B. *Listen to the words with the ch sound. Repeat the words.*

chair	watch	choose
check	itch	

C. *Listen and circle the word you hear.*

1. share
2. choose
3. watch
4. dish

Chapter 8: **Health and Safety**

Page 143 (Chapter Opening)

Listen *Listen and point to the words you hear. Then point to each item in the picture. Listen again and repeat each word.*

1. receptionist
2. cough
3. medicine
4. sore throat
5. sneeze
6. backache
7. headache
8. nurse
9. shoulder(s)
10. foot (feet)
11. chest
12. arm(s)
13. head
14. back
15. leg(s)
16. hand(s)
17. stomach
18. doctor
19. patient
20. thermometer
21. eye(s)
22. nose
23. mouth
24. throat
25. tooth
26. ear
27. tongue

Listen *Listen to three people make appointments with a doctor. Write each person's name, their problem, and the day and time of their appointment.*

1. Receptionist: Downtown Clinic. May I help you?
Man: I'd like to make an appointment to see the doctor.
Receptionist: What's the problem?
Man: I have a backache. My back really hurts.
Receptionist: The doctor can see you tomorrow at 9:00.
Man: Oh. OK, I guess.
Receptionist: What is your name?
Man: Adam. Adam Frost. That's F-R-O-S-T.
2. Receptionist: Downtown Clinic. May I help you?
Woman: Hi. My name is Makoto Obata. I want to make an appointment with the doctor.
Receptionist: Are you sick?
Woman: Well, I have a bad cough.
Receptionist: The doctor can see you on Tuesday.
Woman: What time?
Receptionist: How about 3:00.
Woman: OK. That sounds good.
Receptionist: How do you spell your last name, Ms. Obata?
Woman: O-B-A-T-A.
3. Receptionist: Downtown Clinic. Can I help you?
Man: Hi. I want to make an appointment for my son to see the doctor.
Receptionist: What's the matter with your son?
Man: He has the flu.
Receptionist: You can bring him in today. The doctor can see him at 4:30.
Man: Great! Thank you very much.
Receptionist: Can you tell me your name?
Man: My name is Franco Bellini.
Receptionist: How do you spell that?
Man: My first name is Franco—F-R-A-N-C-O, and my last name is Bellini— B-E-L-L-I-N-I.

Listen *Listen to each conversation. Write the kind of health or safety worker you hear in each conversation.*

1. Nurse: Step on the scale, please. You weigh 200 pounds. You should lose some weight.
Man: I know. I know.
Nurse: OK. Wait in this room. The doctor will be here in just a minute.
2. Doctor: Lift your shirt, please. OK. Now breathe deeply. Good. Well, your heart sounds strong and healthy.
3. 911 Operator: 911.
Woman: This is an emergency. There's a fire in the house across the street.

911 Operator: What's the address?
Woman: It's 945 Smith Street.
911 Operator: We'll send firefighters right away.
4. Man: Help! Help!
Police officer: What's wrong?
Man: That man has my wallet.
Police officer: You stay here. I'll get him.

Listen and Read *Listen to the story. Then read the story.*

Flu Season at the Domingo House

It is flu season and most of the Domingo family is sick. Juan and Gloria have sore throats. Juan also has a fever. His temperature is 102°. Angela is giving him flu medicine. Gloria's temperature is 98.6°. She doesn't have a fever, but she has a stomachache and a headache. Hector also doesn't feel good. He has the chills and body aches. His arms and legs hurt. His shoulders hurt. His back hurts. Even his eyes hurt.

Angela doesn't have a sore throat or a fever. She is the only healthy person in her family, but Angela is tired. She is tired because she is busy helping all the sick people in her family. She should get more sleep. Oh no! Now Angela is sneezing . . . and coughing. Angela is getting sick too!

Pronunciation: *Two sounds of* th

A. th *can sound like the* th *in father. Listen and repeat the words with this* th *sound.*

the   father   that   these

B. th *can sound like the* th *in mouth. Listen and repeat the words with this* th *sound.*

thing   health   mouth   thin

C. *Listen and mark "X" next to the correct pronunciation of* th *in each word you hear.*

__this   __thirty   __throat   __mother
__bath   __teeth   __then   __those

Chapter 9: **Food**

Listen *Listen and point to the words you hear. Then point to each item in the picture. Listen again and repeat each word.*

1. soup
2. sandwich
3. chicken
4. rice
5. salad
6. hamburger
7. french fries
8. bun
9. ketchup
10. soda
11. spaghetti
12. milk
13. waiter

14. cake
15. pie
16. ice cream
17. banana
18. eggs
19. bacon
20. sausage
21. pancakes
22. orange juice
23. waitress
24. coffee
25. check
26. tip
27. menu

Page 168 (Lesson 2, Activity 1)

Listen *Listen and write the names of these vegetables in the picture:* lettuce, corn, tomatoes, potatoes, carrots, onions, mushrooms, broccoli, cucumbers, green beans

1. Woman: How much is the lettuce?
Man: Seventy-nine cents each.
2. Woman: How much is the corn?
Man: They're fifty-nine cents each.
3. Woman: How much are the onions?
Man: They're ninety-nine cents a pound.
4. Woman: How much are the potatoes?
Man: They're sixty-nine cents a pound.
5. Woman: How much are the tomatoes?
Man: They're $1.49 a pound.
6. Woman: How much are the carrots?
Man: They're eighty-nine cents a bunch.
7. Woman: How much are the mushrooms?
Man: They're $2.49 a pound.
8. Woman: How much is the broccoli?
Man: It's ninety-nine cents a pound.
9. Woman: How much are the cucumbers?
Man: They are two for one dollar.
10. Woman: How much are the green beans?
Man: They're $1.05 a pound.

Page 174 (Lesson 3, Activity 2)

Listen *Listen to each customers' order. Check the boxes next to the foods and drinks you hear.*

1. Waitress: Can I take your order?
Man: Yes, please. I'd like the fish special.
Waitress: OK.
Man: And I'd like a cup of chicken soup.
Waitress: Anything to drink?
Man: A cup of coffee with milk, please.
2. Waiter: Are you ready to order?
Woman: Yes, I think so.
Waiter: What would you like?
Woman: I'd like a chicken sandwich. I'd also like a small salad with that.
Waiter: OK. And what would you like to drink?
Woman: I'd like apple juice.
Waiter: I'm sorry. We don't have apple juice.
Woman: OK, then I'll have orange juice.
3. Waitress: What can I get you?
Woman: What's your lunch special?

Waitress: The special is a hamburger with french fries.
Woman: Can I get a cheeseburger?
Waitress: Yes. That's not a problem.
Woman: I'd also like extra onions.
Waitress: OK. And what would you like to drink?
Woman: Just a glass of water, please.

Page 180 (Chapter Review)

Pronunciation: *Long* e *and short* e

Listen to the sound of e *in each word and repeat the words. Circle the words with the short* e *sound (as in* egg*) and underline the words with the long* e *sound (as in* beans*).*

ketchup	beef	coffee
tea	menu	check

Chapter 10: **Work**

Page 183 (Chapter Opening)

Listen *Listen and point to the words you hear. Then point to each item in the picture. Listen again and repeat each word.*

1. newspaper
2. "Help Wanted" section
3. advertisement
4. pay
5. interview
6. handshake
7. interviewer
8. application
9. experience
10. skills

Page 191 (Lesson 2, Activity 5)

Listen *Listen to the conversations. Circle the information you hear.*

Conversation 1
Man: Do you have any job openings?
Woman: Yes, we do. We have an opening for a delivery person.
Man: What skills does the job require?
Woman: You must be a good driver.
Man: Do I have to have experience?
Woman: No, no experience is required.
Man: Is it full-time or part-time?
Woman: It's part-time.
Man: What are the days?
Woman: We need someone to work from Wednesday to Saturday.
Man: What are the hours?
Woman: Six o'clock in the morning to one o'clock in the afternoon.
Male: What is the pay?
Female: The pay is $13 per hour, plus benefits.
Male: How can I apply?
Female: You need to call for an appointment. Call 213-555-4565

Conversation 2
Woman 1: What positions do you have open right now?
Woman 2: We have an opening for a receptionist.

Woman 1: Is it a full-time job?
Woman 2: Yes, it is. We need someone from Monday to Friday.
Woman 1: What are the hours?
Woman 2: 8:00 AM to 4:00 PM.
Woman 1: Can you tell me the pay?
Woman 2: The starting pay is $8.50 an hour.
Woman 1: Do I need experience?
Woman 2: Yes, you should have one or two years experience. Also, you need to have good phone skills.
Woman 1: How can I apply?
Woman 2: Come to our office to fill out an application. We're located at 233 Avenue B.

Page 192 (Lesson 2, Activity 7)

Listen *Listen and circle the word you hear.*

1. Man: He is my manager.
2. Man: I work for him.
3. Woman: I was in the office yesterday.
4. Woman: You were with me.
5. Man: She is at work.
6. Man: I'm going to call her.

Page 197 Chapter Review, Activity 1

Listen and Read *Listen to the story. Then read the story.*

Angela's Idea

Angela still wants a new apartment. Hector thinks they don't have enough money, but Angela has an idea. She is going to tell Hector about her idea tonight.

Angela's children are in school now. They don't need her during the day. Angela has time for a job, and she has job skills. She was an office assistant in Mexico. She can use a computer, she can file, and now her English is good enough to answer phones and take messages.

Today there are some interesting "Help Wanted" ads in the newspaper. One ad is for a receptionist job at the Downtown Computer Store. The ad says, "Some experience necessary." It also says "apply in person."

Tomorrow she is going to go to the store and get an application. She is going to tell them about her skills and her work experience in Mexico. Maybe they will hire her, and maybe they won't. But she is going to try.

Angela is excited. This is the start of a new adventure in her new country!

Page 200 (Chapter Review)

Pronunciation: /s/ and /th/

A. *Listen and repeat the pairs of words.*

sing / thing
sick / thick
sank / thank
saw / thaw
sigh / thigh
sin / thin

B. *Say one word from each of the word pairs in Activity A to a partner. Ask your partner to point to the word you say.*

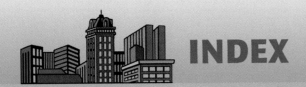

INDEX

ACADEMIC SKILLS

INDEX

LIFE SKILLS

INDEX

TOPICS

 **INDEX**

WORKFORCE SKILLS